Loneliness

Adam Bittleston

Loneliness

Floris Books

First published in 1987 by Floris Books, Edinburgh

British Library CIP Data

Bittleston, Adam
Loneliness.
1. Loneliness—Religious aspects—Christianity
I. Title
248.4   BV4911

ISBN 0-86315-056-X

Printed in Great Britain
by Billing & Sons Ltd, Worcester

Contents

1. The onset of loneliness

Someone in acute pain rarely asks for a book about pain. It is relief from pain that is called for, if possible the removal of the cause. Someone in acute loneliness does not want to discuss what loneliness is, but needs the right kind of company. Nevertheless this book may have its uses. It may contribute, for those who do not feel lonely, towards their understanding for loneliness in others, and particularly towards seeing how deep and complex its roots are — so that they may be less inclined to feel a slight contempt for the lonely and be better able to help. For human beings are very much inclined to feel a little contemptuous about people in trouble. This is of course very marked with mental illness; the older words for this condition are all used in a thoroughly derogatory sense and even those suffering in this way are inclined to despise themselves. So it is, though in a less obvious way, with loneliness; if we hear of somebody else's loneliness, we are inclined to feel that the person concerned is in some way to blame. And we do not readily acknowledge ourselves to be lonely.

Nevertheless what may seem to be a surprising number of people who live alone do say, if they are approached by a sympathetic listener, that they are lonely, even desperately lonely. This is not an experience that can be measured; but the relatively few people who have done research in this field have come up with some remarkable results. For example it seems that among those living alone the highest incidence of loneliness is among those around forty years old, not as perhaps would be expected among those of sixty or seventy. People living alone suffer both in the country and in the town; and this has measurable effects on physical health, particularly on heart disease. It seems widely agreed that suffering through loneliness is on the increase in our society, and that not nearly enough is done about it, though considerable efforts are being made, often by young people.

But it is by no means only those who live alone who are lonely. Perhaps nearly everyone, at some time of their lives and on some level of their being, has this pain. Some people who appear very busy, with a lively and friendly family, may feel deeply that the contacts they have do not come near to satisfying some of their needs to communicate. The novelist, Georgette Heyer, had a devoted husband who was very interested in her work, a loving son and daughter-in-law, many thousands of readers who were enthusiastic about her romantic but discerning historical comedies, but her biographer says that in her later years she suffered from loneliness.

Why was this? I believe it was because she was a true artist, in her special field. People enjoy being entertained; but they very seldom realize how difficult the entertainer's art is. Actors are drawn to parts in tragedy — but parts in true comedy really demand much more of their abilities. A multitude of Georgette Heyer's readers appreciated the romantic story; many too had a sense of the scrupulous care she gave to historical detail, particularly in language. But it seems that very few appreciated her as an artist – not even she herself. She often wrote scornfully about her own work — as some very great artists have done. She needed a few other loving artists to talk to.

Not long ago a man died who for many years had done very good work as a doctor. He was surrounded by affection, both from his patients and those who worked with him. His work was regarded by many as remarkably

8

successful; but he held that certain methods of treatment widely used today are both harmful in the long run and morally wrong. He tried to persuade as many doctors as he could of this; and he was almost entirely unsuccessful. On *this* level of his being, which was very important for him, his last years were lonely and unhappy.

It takes courage, and a sustained effort towards self-knowledge to look back on one's life and see how different kinds of loneliness developed. But it is worth doing this, not only for its effect on oneself but also as a help towards understanding others. The very beginning of loneliness lies indeed beyond the reach of our normal memories; it is at the moment of birth, when we were separated from the close enfolding of our mother's body and perhaps the sound of her heartbeat. At once the attempt to communicate begins, in cries of dissatisfaction and intent listening for voices; and the failure to achieve results by communication begins too.

In this book the view will be taken that the events of pregnancy and birth are not an absolute beginning, but the continuation of a long story, which leads back into worlds of spirit and earlier lives on earth. This is not just an arbitrary fancy; it was the general view of a great part of humanity until comparatively recently. It has been confirmed in our century by the careful, deeply conscientious spiritual research of Rudolf Steiner; and most people who are prepared to give attention to this conception of the nature of man, by looking at the events and experiences of their own and other people's lives will find, I believe, that it sheds a flood of light on them.

The spiritual world from which our souls descended into earth was very rich in communication. There we listened, not from outside, but as if indwelling the beings called in the oldest Christian tradition the hierarchies of angels.

To help us to communicate on earth, we have to use our

physical senses, most obviously hearing and sight. And at first we interpret what we hear and see very imperfectly. In some ways this may hold true all through life. People differ in the languages they use and the ways in which they use them. And people vary in their gestures and the expressions of their faces. Children imitate their speech and their expressions; they also begin quite soon to reject what is said and to ask questions. Often their reasons for contradicting are not understood, and their questions are not answered. (I can remember being scolded when small for 'answering back'. How else, I wondered, could one answer but 'back'?)

From such failures in communication the sense of individuality may well develop. 'This is me, who has not been understood; this is me, who wants to know, and is not told.' The grown-ups are either very stupid or very ill-informed about such subjects, for example, as why grass is green and time keeps on getting later. No questions asked by a child are really senseless; generally they hide some aspect of the difference between the spiritual world and this earthly world. Sometimes the mother, or someone else, comes up with a deeply satisfying answer. But in general the stronger the sense of having come from another realm is in the child, the more likely it is that questions will be given up altogether, or wait for many years until the right teacher is found. Meanwhile there is much loneliness.

But estrangement may also develop not because the child's soul is different from those of its family and neighbours, but because they find something unusual in the child's body. Merciless eyes often spot very small things which need not be regarded as offensive in themselves, but seem to call for ridicule simply because they are different, for example, to have eyes of different colours. On matters of this kind no satisfactory communication at all may prove possible.

1. THE ONSET OF LONELINESS

Through entry into the physical world, we have taken on the earthly senses. These tell us about the great world around us and about the seemingly little world which we are — though it too is really boundless. They consist not only in the familiar senses of touch and smell and taste and sight and hearing, but also of senses which reveal conditions in our own body or of the finer qualities in what is said and thought in our environment. Rudolf Steiner has shown that they form something like a great ring of twelve, each having qualities which resemble but differ from those of its immediate neighbours.

The condition and the good development of our senses have a great deal to do with the experience of loneliness; and it is here that we shall begin a study in some detail of the circumstances which help to bring about loneliness, and the measures which can do much to heal it. Only after this we shall go on to consider relationships within families and their effect on our later ability to communicate with human beings in general. But people do not only need people; the finer development of the senses enables us to approach a realm little regarded by most adults at the present time, whose inhabitants would very much like to establish communication with us — the realm of elemental beings. Through study of the family we shall be led to consider another great company with whom our communications have largely broken down: the host of human beings who have gone through death. And finally we may try to look at the way in which all these beings on earth and in the heavens have developed in the past and are developing and will develop in the present and in the future, with the human experience of loneliness as a necessary stage on the journey.

2. The ring of the senses

In the first years of childhood, the use of the senses develops rapidly. And a great many of the attempts at communication between child and adult are concerned with this development. It is very important for the child to discover how adults respond to this wonderful new shared world. And yet its own experiences are often in marked contrast with those of the adult. Small children, for example, very often like mud; adults often noticeably less. Countless problems of this sort encounter the small child. They are compensated for by shared joys, as when an adult can dance with the child. Most of the happy process of learning names for things helps in communicating pleasures and distastes.

From very early on, however, individual differences in the use of the senses have their effects. The child may have an impaired sense organ or an exceptionally delicate one. Either of these leads very often to loneliness. People irritate each other by responding differently to a sight or a sound or a smell — or not perceiving it at all. And this irritation is noticeable. If we want to train ourselves to understand and to like other people with whom we have to do, it can be good to ask ourselves about the quality of their sense-perceptions, and their response to them. Some people bring into their perceiving of the world much more from the life before birth than others. They may be deeply moved, though unable to explain it, by the wonderful difference between what a thing looked like from the spiritual world and its appearance on earth. (An outstanding example is the child diarist Opal Whiteley who, brought up by uncomprehending foster-parents, could write in her secret solitude of 'the star-songs of the potato'!)

All the senses depend upon our possession of the physical body and convey to us facts and events of the physical world — though some of them appear much nearer to spiritual reality than others. Rudolf Steiner on a number of occasions spoke or wrote of the twelve senses in this order:

Touch
Life
Movement
Balance
Smell
Taste
Sight
Warmth
Hearing
Speech
Thought
'I'

Some of these will need a good deal of explaining when we come to them. We can regard this sequence as an ascent — but also as a ring with the sense of touch as neighbour to the sense of another person's 'I'. And for the purpose of relating the senses with the experience of loneliness, we may begin with the sense of life and end with the sense of touch.

From life-sense to warmth

Through the life-sense we are aware whether our own body feels well and energetic or tired and in need of rest. The life-sense tends to be noticeable at the extremes; many people, for most of their lives, feel neither a surplus of energy nor a painful lack of it. Some people are so convinced and satisfied about their own health that they are strongly inclined to despise anyone who feels tired or ill. There are others who at least for long periods of their lives hardly ever feel well, whose life-sense is always indicating a flagging body. Such marked differences contribute immediately to a sense of loneliness — in general in the one who feels tired while everyone else seems abounding in strength. In pain or grave illness the soul may feel deeply isolated, imprisoned in the body. And it may find that hardly anyone has any vivid sense of what its condition is like, except those who are actually suffering from the same thing at the same time, as sometimes in a hospital ward. Among these an alleviating feeling of companionship can grow up, as among the groups of lepers who wandered through many regions during the Middle Ages and earlier.

There are more delicate differences in the experience brought to us through the life sense because we inhabit different bodies. It is not the same to live in a tall, thin body, or in a small, stout one. The harmony or disharmony of proportion is observed not only outwardly by those who see us, but also inwardly through our sense of life. We can try to be aware not only of what our own life-sense is expressing from time to time, but of some, both of the long-term and the short-term experiences, of others. Some people who are extremely stout, for instance, may become very much accustomed to their condition, though a continuous nagging complaint by their life-sense is going on, rising to an angry protest when they climb a hill on a hot day. All through life some degree of communication about such things, though perhaps only with those near to us, may mean very much.

The sense of movement and the sense of balance are intimately related and can be taken together here. Again, we may feel ourselves happily part of a community when our movements and our awareness of carrying them out are much the same as those of the people around us. But a small child can feel lonely if he notices that other children can walk and run when such movements have not yet been achieved by him. Later on a human being who walks or moves unsteadily or clumsily, or for whom some kinds of movement are impossible, may be stricken with acute loneliness. The child who walks along the top of a wall or who learns to ride a bicycle, can have a great joy in his sense of balance; when this is impaired, even if only for a brief period, it is as if something of our central human dignity is threatened. But being able to run down a grassy slope together or to skate as a group, can be a great and shining joy.

With the senses of smell, taste and sight we pass over the threshold of our own bodily organism and enter into the qualities of the external world. It need not delay us here that philosophers and others have often regarded the sensations of smell, taste and colour as purely subjective. In reality there is nothing in our experience which is totally subjective or totally objective; everywhere world and human being meet and contribute their part. In general, experiences of pleasure or disgust through the senses of smell and taste are very intensely shared, especially by children. A big dining-room where many children are eating can be hushed for a time by delight in a very satisfactory puddings. As we grow older, our experience of differences in taste may become more particular, though it does not generally pervade our whole organism in the same way as earlier. A baby's pleasure in his mother's milk — or perhaps his dissatisfaction if something seems wrong with it — fills him utterly. Later, he may feel the encounter with a strange taste — for example that of cheese or of an olive — as a whole disaster, down to his toes.

Both children and grown-ups with unspoilt natural feel-

15

ings find in a good meal, with a variety of tastes and aromas, something of the bounty of a kind mother, indeed of Mother Earth herself. This is not just a poetical expression; there is indeed such a Mother, and a sensitive appreciation of the world of nature leads towards her. The rich world of tastes and smells and colours contains everywhere the traces of the elemental beings, whose good representatives are her faithful and conscious servants. Even today these beings are often seen by children, and their presence and activity felt by grown people. Our emotional responses to sense impressions are often influenced by the relationship of the elemental beings to processes going on around us, whether naturally or as a result of human technology. If we take fairly simple and familiar processes as examples, probably almost everyone is encouraged by the smell of newly baked bread or discouraged by the smell of burnt porridge or burning rubber. In regions where factories discharge their effluents and waste products during the night hours, most of the inhabitants sleep with their windows shut. But if one happened to want fresh air at three or four in the morning, the atmosphere brought a very hostile answer indeed. And this could bring people sensitive to such things near to despair, as if they were wrestling with an opponent much too strong for them.

Some of the elementals who serve the great Mother can be distinguished into four categories, the gnomes, the undines, the sylphs, and the fire spirits, working respectively in the 'elements' — or conditions of matter — of earth, water, air and warmth, and in the encounters of each of these with each other. Many flavours and aromas testify to the working of undines and sylphs in plants, for instance in the astonishing chemistry of leaf and flower, and this work of theirs goes over into the realm of colour.

But perhaps the most detailed and convincing description of the elemental beings written in recent years is by a woman who never saw colours with her eyes. Ursula Burkhard's book *Karlik* is very instructive both about loneliness and about companionship.

Ursula Burkhard was born, and has remained, totally blind. Her earliest childhood memories are not only of the company of human beings, but also of elemental beings, who brought her much happiness. When she could speak, she often told about them, and the grown-up people who heard her were at first pleased, and thought that she possessed a remarkable power of fantasy. But as she grew older, they saw that she was absolutely assured of this other world's reality. Then they tried to convince her that it was all illusion, and even told her that since there was nothing in the Bible about such beings, to believe in them was a sin. It was hard for her to accept that while she had to believe in so many things the grown-ups told her that were beyond *her* experience, what she herself experienced, and they did not, must be nonsensical or sinful. But under the pressure she did turn away her attention from the elemental beings until the time came when she ceased to accept the religious views of her elders. Then she could open again her spiritual senses to the rich, lively, industrious world of these elementals, who were willing to teach her a great deal. She came to understand their connections with stone, plant, animal and man, and their entirely different relationship to things which seem in the human mind so fixed and definite, for example number and size. Elementals do not have a measurable size or position. In *Karlik* Ursula Burkhard is at pains to make clear how different the perceptions of their world are from physical sense-impressions. She calls to her help, in describing this difference, Rudolf Steiner's use of the words Imagination, Inspiration and Intuition.

What she describes is entirely based on her own experience. The loneliness natural to an extremely independent-minded and gifted blind person has received some comfort, it seems, from having found human beings who at least recognize the existence of the elementals — although this belief if it remains only theoretical may not prevent them from inflicting grave harm on the elementals by their thoughts, words and deeds. Nevertheless, many among the elemental beings have great hopes of future friendships with humans. And human beings may come to feel their own hours of loneliness as gifts of destiny, calling them to deepen their awareness of such boundlessly wonderful and helpful potential companions.

It is useful, on the way towards awareness of the elemental beings, for a person with the ordinary sense of sight to realize that impressions of colour should not be regarded as *separate* in the way that particular flavours or scents can be regarded as being (though man-made scents are often made by blending a great number of ingredients). What we experience as a colour and tend to ascribe to a particular object, say a red pillar-box or a blue carpet, is really the result of a complex interplay between one or more sources of light, a surface and all the other surfaces from which it receives reflected light, and the viewer. The green of the leaf, for example, is different in midday, or morning, or evening light, under a clear or cloudy sky, in a garden, in a park, or in a street. Such differences may seem unimportant, and we speak bluntly of a white rose, although we have never seen such a thing. It matters very much for the human soul that colours are always influencing one another, like human beings in earnest conversation. The great Mother never forgets that she has many children, and considers them all wisely, helping to develop among them good relationships.

But though the sense of sight is such a subtle thing it contributes more than any other sense to our feeling that we share as human beings in a common world. Thus the

onset of blindness may bring a very great shock. A man
has described how he suddenly became blind in the middle
of a busy London railway station and asked for help from
person after person. Each one simply went away and did
not come back. His blindness proved incurable, and his
grief about it was embittered by this initial experience of
indifference and rejection. But it is often astonishing to see
how well blind people compensate for their deprivation.
An example known to many is that of the French writer
Jacques Lusseyran, whose blindness was caused by an
accident in a schoolroom when he was a boy, and who
gradually formed new kinds of personal relationships with
the help of an awakening vision which was not dependent
upon physical eyes.

Within months of his accident he realized that he could
now see colours and movements which revealed a great
deal about the people round him, and other living things —
for example, trees by the roadside. He saw what are sometimes called 'auras'. This power of seeing decreased if he
was himself angry or afraid. But it became so reliable
and exact that when he became a member of the French
Resistance during the Second World War, he was asked to
assess the characters of many who applied to participate
in the Resistance, using this special power of his. Could
the applicant be trusted? Many people's lives might depend
on his answer. For a considerable time everything went
well; but one day he was uncertain, and gave the applicant
the benefit of the doubt. He proved mistaken, and he
himself and many of his associates were arrested and put
into concentration camps. But he survived, and could
devote his life to working for the blind in many countries,
encouraging employers to discover how much the blind
can do.

Not very many of the blind, perhaps, will develop at
present their power of inner vision to the degree achieved

by Lusseyran. But all of them, whether blind from birth or having developed blindness, can grow more aware of the inner light that they have and that it can be fostered.

Lusseyran found, as other blind people do, that he could strengthen his feeling of belonging to a common physical world by using his other senses to an exceptional extent, for example the sense of touch.

One of the ways in which the blind are deprived is their inability to see the colours of the skins and hair, eyes and clothes of other people. The clothes people wear are an important means of non-verbal communication, even sometimes a cry for help. A woman may wear shabby brown and grey clothes to signal that she no longer feels herself of value in the world and has largely abandoned the attempt to communicate what is important to her. Someone may be either frustrated or inwardly supported by having to wear a uniform. In many ways someone can be hindered from wearing the clothes in which she or he would feel happy and visible, by circumstances, for instance by inheriting the clothes of older brothers and sisters, or by poverty. (Elisabeth Kübler Ross as a child was obliged to wear identical clothes with her twin sister, from whom she felt very different, thus increasing what she felt as the stupid inability of friends, or even members of the family, to distinguish between them.) Or a person may be to some extent colour-blind, or with little sense of how colours go together or express character.

On the other hand, the sense of sight may become too intensive and even disturbing. A patient's health in hospital may be rendered worse by the colour of his room. A remarkable, and indeed unique, example can be found in the life of Kaspar Hauser, who was found poorly dressed and hardly able to walk or speak, on the streets of Nürnberg in 1828 at the age of about sixteen. His origin has never been completely proved but an enormous amount of research over the last hundred and fifty years has indicated that he was the son of the Grand Duke of Baden and his wife Stephanie, the adopted daughter of Napoleon. It appears that a short time after his birth a dying child was substituted for him without his mother's knowledge; and that he was then looked after secretly, for fourteen years or so, in a cell in semi-darkness, where he was fed only on bread and water, and was without any human contact until shortly before his release. Nobody knows for certain who his captors were, or their motives. But the story of his imprisonment is confirmed in its essentials by the detailed anatomical reports made by a physician while he was still in police custody in Nürnberg.

Kaspar Hauser had thus suffered an extraordinary deprivation in the life of his senses over a long period of his childhood and youth. This showed itself in many ways. He could see the colours of objects undiscernible by others at a distance at night, but at first the sight of an open view in daylight was extremely painful and indeed horrible for him. As he began to distinguish and name the colours, he could say that the greenness of trees seemed to him ugly. The smell of alcohol, even many yards away, made him very unwell. On the other hand, he was very much impressed by the colour of people's clothes and particularly by military uniforms. His memory was extraordinary; quite soon when he had become well-known in Nürnberg and was visited by eighty or ninety people a day, he could recall the names, positions, and clothes of every person.

He was released by the police, and cared for by an extraordinary group of gifted and distinguished men who made his case known, not only in Nürnberg, but very widely throughout Europe. The utterly isolated boy became the object of love and concern for thousands of people of all classes. Members of the many royal families of the time, of the aristocracy, of the professional classes,

21

and the humblest working people wanted him to be helped and protected. He was a classless being, appalled by any form of violence, gentle and affectionate, with a kind of paradisal innocence. After five and a half years he was mortally wounded. He died in a mood of complete forgiveness towards his unknown enemies, saying that no-one had harmed him.

Kaspar Hauser had a strong attachment to animals, particularly horses; and though we depend very much in our knowledge of animals upon sight, blind or partially sighted people can find a great deal of comfort in the friendships that can grow up for them with animals. And wherever an attachment exists between a man and an animal — not only with pet animals but among farmers and shepherds who know their herds or flocks by name — another being is present invisibly but very actively, belonging to the order of fire spirits or salamanders.

These are beings of great constructive will; they are present, for instance, wherever the ripening process is going on in nourishing plants. To have their help we do not need to adopt a pet animal; we can call upon their help quite simply when we have physical difficulty in standing up, from lying or sitting, and their help will probably come. They are concerned particularly with our waking hours, and bring us good ideas, while the undines like to weave in our dreams. It is good to seek their company particularly in the part of the year between Easter and midsummer when a gentle warmth is encouraging the opening of flowers.

Here a close neighbour of the sense of sight, the sense for warmth and cold, comes into play. This is seldom impaired, even in fever or hypothermia; its organs are spread out over the whole skin. It establishes a comparison between the temperature of the human being and the temperature surrounding him. If anything is some degrees below average skin temperature, it is felt as cold; if it is some degrees above it, it is felt as warm. Skin temperature is a little below basic bodily temperature, which is nearly identical in human beings all over the earth. We are astonishingly self-regulating, exposed to wide differences of temperature in different climatic conditions. It seems that human beings are rather more sensitive to cold than animals, though many animals are extremely happy about their own or external warmth.

But here we meet particularly the prejudice that only the measurable is real. Just as it is thought that colours are mostly differences in the wavelengths of light, it is thought that warmth and cold are simply the differences indicated by thermometers. But warmth, like everything else, is a manifestation of being, of soul. It has qualitative as well as quantitative differences. The light from the television set has a measurably different set of wavelengths from the sunlight. Many people today are exposed for hours to a different light-diet from that of the age-old nourishment provided by sun, moon, stars and firelight. And an electric heater does not provide the same warmth as candles do, though this difference in quality may not be measurable (given enough candles). Human social life depends upon right temperatures, quantitatively and qualitatively. People subject to very cold conditions become uncommunicative, in general, and those who are warmer, up to a certain point, more voluble. It is a social disaster when people live in houses or rooms which they cannot make warm enough. And so it is when they have a work in which not enough social warmth is developed, or no satisfying work at all.

We should never lose hold of the fact that human beings need real contact and communication with other people, and nothing replaces this. But periods of isolation can be regarded positively, and not simply as misfortunes. We have in English the beautiful word 'solitude'; many people feel this word as describing something to be valued and put to good use. In no solitude are we in reality alone. We are granted the opportunity of cultivating our relationship with other beings and what are ordinarily regarded as things. Among visible living beings, we have not only animals but also plants and trees. It should not be considered as sentimentality or superstition if it is said that a kind of communication, appreciated on both sides, can be established with plants and flowers. Careful and precise experiments have even been made under the same conditions of temperature, humidity and so on, but surrounded by different sounds. Repeatedly, the plants which grew best were those spoken to in a friendly way by human beings. There appear also to have been marked differences between plants exposed (if that is the right word) to different kinds of music. In recent years there has been an enormous increase in potted plants kept indoors, and many people notice how these flourish if talked to, though it is not quite easy to do so aloud without feeling ridiculous. A stream of warm appreciation between human being and plant has its worth not only in the moment, or within the life-time of the plant, but lastingly in invisible worlds. And we need not think only of the living plant; someone who works with a material derived from a plant, quite particularly wood, may feel a living relationship to its source. Not so long ago, Japanese joiners and carpenters took into consideration the direction in which the wood they were using had stood in the tree from which it came, and felt that if they did not, this might bring misfortune to the house where they were working.

Perhaps almost everyone knows that solitude in the open air, in beautiful country or by the sea, can bring very special blessings, though it may be awkward, if other people look at us enquiringly or even suspiciously. The moving air becomes alive for us and the song of wild birds can begin to reveal what they have learned from the sylphs. It is only in our heads that we are so cut off from the elementals; from the shoulders down we are always dimly aware of them. And in the open we can try to converse with their multitudes.

There is a wonderful old Irish fairy story about a hunchback basket weaver called Lusmore (the name of a flower he often wears in his hat) who lives in a village. One night he is walking home laboriously up a long hill, after selling his baskets in a neighbouring town. He is quite alone. At length he comes to a lake close to a deserted castle. Here he sits down for a little to rest. Presently he begins to hear singing, which is not from human voices. Over and over again the words are sung, 'Monday, Tuesday, Monday, Tuesday . . .'. After a time he gently sings back to them, in his tuneful voice, continuing their melody: 'And what about Wednesday? And what about Wednesday?' The singers were water spirits or undines, and they are delighted with this human contribution. Their leader comes to speak with Lusmore, and as a token of friendship heals his hump. Now he can walk easily and hardly knows how he gets home. This event becomes widely known, and another man with a hump, who is neither tactful nor tuneful, comes to ask how it happened. *His* meeting with the water spirits is not so happy, and he receives a second hump, which he will have to keep — unless Lusmore helps him.

This story contains much wisdom. The good elementals would like to establish closer, more conscious relationships with humanity. Their desire for this can really be compared with human loneliness; though it is a need for companionship with another kind of being, not with each other. It is a deep, compelling wish, a sense of incompleteness and unfulfilment. If mankind were to go on ignoring this need, it would be like the behaviour of a bad neighbour, disregarding mortal trouble next door. If we deepen our feelings about even the simplest rhythms of life, we are coming to meet them. The rhythms of day and year are evident examples.

But the rhythm of the week is also an image of great cosmic rhythms, and we can begin to feel the different quality in each day. These are qualities which have been associated since ancient times with the planets: Saturn, Sun, Moon, Mars, Mercury, Jupiter, Venus. If the world were to stop at Tuesday, physical conflict and violence would go on. Wednesday, Mercury's day, is the day of the spirit of healing, in Christian language the day of Raphael. About Raphael there is a wonderful, and all too seldom read, story in the Old Testament: the Book of Tobit. (Some Bibles relegate this to the Apocrypha or leave it out altogether.) The Archangel Raphael in the form of a man accompanies the young Tobias on a long and difficult journey, and as they pause beside a river helps him to catch a large and terrifying fish which can later be used for purposes of healing.

Beside a river . . . Wherever there are frontiers between water and the other elements the undines are particularly near and approachable. But they do not like such frontiers to be straight, and in nature they seldom are. It is man who has a strong, and often unfortunate, addiction to straight lines, and often imprisons water in pipes and canals; though he makes up for this to some small extent with some beautiful fountains. Water likes to leap, and be illumined. There was a very gifted Dutch teacher who asserted, and believed, that there is no such thing as bad weather. Frits Julius would stand happily beside a grassy bank pointing out to drenched students, who did not entirely share his views, the magnificent variety of plants growing there. He wrote inspiring books about plants and stars and human character but his principal work was to teach children in a school founded on the teachings of Rudolf Steiner in the Hague. He knew about the interest taken by gnomes and undines in stories about young children. And he had a friend who told him that he had been helped by gnomes to find crystals. But he did not follow up these indications actively until he was staying with a party of young people in south-west Switzerland, and ate too much whipped cream. As a result he had to be left behind one morning when the rest of the party went on an expedition among the peaks. He remained behind feeling lonely and resentful. But he decided that if the others could go up he could go down. What followed can be quoted in his own words at some length.

I had no people to walk with — well then, I would choose the nature spirits, and perhaps they would be better company. 'If that fellow got enough contact with the nature-spirits for him to find crystals, they are sure to show me something too.' In a few seconds all my rancour and jealousy were transformed into a shining optimism. I opened the door and stood on the steps, calling to my mind the best memory pictures I had of small children, inviting the gnomes and undines as if I were calling children to a meal. And, O wonder, I walked then for three hours, without taking any step which was not led. Without actually seeing much of them, I had the whole time a very definite feeling, as if two gnomes-like beings were taking me with them by the hand. I noticed always through a gentle pressure or pull, impressions that were more moral than mechanical, what their intentions were. Everything depended on careful attentiveness on my side. However strongly and often I was guided, there was not the slightest

compulsion. I had to think again and again
how much we lose through not being attentive
enough.

First we went up, and then across a sunlit
meadow, zig-zagging from flower to flower. It was
already far into the autumn, and I had not yet
looked at any flower there. Thus to my great
astonishment they did not show me crystals, but
flowers. It seemed as if they had made a quick
agreement: 'This one here thinks he knows
something about plants. We shall let him look for
once at what he never sees.' Then we went down
to a stream between steep banks. I was put in
front of a huge flat rock and made to look. There
was a great cleft in the rock, and in it stood a tiny
tree. With other small plants, it gave the impression
of a miniature garden. When I had expressed
inwardly that I had seen and admired it I was led
further. This showed clearly that these beings very
much appreciate interest in their tasks and
concerns. In *Man as Symphony* Rudolf Steiner
speaks of mediation between plant roots and the
mineral realm as one of the main tasks of the
gnomes. Where can this be better seen than in such
a place, where rock is loosened and softened, to
become accessible for plants? Later on, they often
put me in front of some nearly bare stone, on
which only a few little plants were growing, or
where a patch of moss was beginning to claim its
place. They like to point out where there is a breath
of moss even on walls along streets in our towns.
Another important task for the gnomes is to awaken
life in the seed and push the first shoots up into
the light. So one can understand why later on they
drew my attention not only to many stones but to

bare places in woods, where perhaps a single plant was beginning to grow. And later on it became very significant to observe repeatedly what I noticed on this first walk — how something can appear like a beautifully arranged garden.

Even someone who cannot achieve, or does not wish for, the kind of social dealings with nature-spirits touched on here, may observe the visible things here described and make surprising discoveries. And some contact with these beings is really coming about, directly one concerns oneself with their activities.

When we had finished with the rock I was led quickly to a place on the bank of the stream opposite a thickly grown island. The water was quite wide but I was directed to cross it. I resisted this — Steiner speaks of gnomes that play tricks! But I was persuaded, and with the help of a stepping-stone crossed dry-shod. (Similar things often happened later.) On the island I was led a devious path, and shown several instructive things. Delightedly they pointed out a tall plant with brilliant autumn colours, while everything else was still dull green. I asked myself — how can a gnome, who lives generally within solid things, be interested in my impression of the colour of a plant? But this helped me especially to understand that the world is a scene enacted *for us*. As with a play, we should not hope to find the essential reality *behind* the scenes (as science too often does) — behind theatrical scenery there is generally ugliness. Just as with a play the performance is the main thing, to which everything else is subordinate; nature itself is a performance that is only successful if we look at it in the right way. If we understand this, the whole world becomes different for us.

During the whole excursion I had looked ahead as little as possible, not to be distracted by questions of direction. And on the island I could not even see immediately ahead, it was such a tangle. At last I was led firmly towards the water, and began to wonder about reaching the further bank. But just where I reached the water there was a plank on which I could cross. This did not solve everything. The bank was a swamp — but I let myself be led by a zig-zag, without looking round anxiously for something better, to firm ground. Then there was a steep slope, to be negotiated by the ordinary public only on hands and feet. But I was brought like a guest of honour to a natural staircase, plain but secret, that I could ascend royally upright.

Later on I often encountered much worse bogs, which I would never have been able to cross without help. If I let myself be led, I found the most unlikely ways through. There are paths everywhere, that are visible when pointed out — but they never go in straight lines.

Again I was led to the bank of the stream — and there I had to stop for a long time. Several times already I had been held up, where there was nothing conspicuous to be seen. I understood this as a wish for more stories, and when I had complied the expedition went on. But there was nothing fresh to be seen here, and stories had no effect. I accepted imprisonment and waited for my destiny. Above the ridge of the mountain on the other side the light was becoming more intense, and the white flaming edge of the sun emerged from the dark rock. This produced a mood of incredible festivity in the water rushing and leaping over the stones. This what what I had to see. Everywhere gleaming sparks, interweaving, being mirrored, suddenly darkened. This was the climax of my expedition—which was, all of it, a festival. But how was this possible? It is a difficult job to be a guide — how could these beings be so good at it?

That day my gnome university was only just beginning. The indications were always of the kind I have described. The picture appeared magically in one's mind, or outside — the rest one had to do oneself. However simple the indications often were in themselves, they might point to far-reaching connections, even glimpses of the past and future of the earth.

Such an expedition brings about an extraordinary mood. One loses connection with time, and one's entire surroundings take on a fairy-tale quality. One is led into a strange kingdom. Yet on such paths I have never seen anything that could not be seen by anyone — though perhaps things that nobody has ever seen.*

From hearing to the sense of touch

Not without reason, on the journey round the ring of the senses, have we paused in the realm of sight and the experience of warmth. To reach the remaining senses we have to cross a threshold. Hearing, the sense for speech, the sense for thoughts, and the 'I'-sense are all very directly concerned in communication. They admit us into the interior of the things and beings around us though still

* *The Golden Blade 1971*, pp. 131–35.

remaining at first in the physical world. To hear anything at all is much more than we realize a kind of miracle. Rudolf Steiner has described how with sight and the feeling of warmth we can send out corresponding elements of our own being to meet the revelation of nature. But with hearing we need the special help of a being much greater and wiser than ourselves – a being of the hierarchy of angels. With extraordinary selflessness, he helps us to enter into the wonderfully diversified world of sound, and to feel deeply about its gifts. An impairment in the sense of sound is felt very strongly as a cause of loneliness, for which it is by no means easy to compensate. It is not often noticed how even partial deafness, including deafness in one ear, makes it much more difficult to participate where several conversations are going on close together in the same room. In children partial deafness is often not noticed until astonishingly late, long after it has become a cause of loneliness.

In the history of Europe, and perhaps in the history of the world, we have the greatest example of deafness in Beethoven. Sometimes people have wished that as little about his personal life had come to be known as about Shakespeare's. But the very detailed picture given by his biographers can also be regarded as deeply relevant to the appreciation of his music, and as illuminating many problems to be found in human nature generally.

His deafness came on gradually from about the age of twenty-four. In the Heiligenstadt Testament addressed to his brothers, he wrote:

> Only consider that for six years I have been
> suffering an incurable affliction, aggravated by
> imprudent physicians . . . all with a fiery impulsive
> temperament, sensible, even, to the distractions of
> social life. I was yet compelled early in my life to
> isolate myself, to spend my life in solitude . . . Oh,
> how could I possibly admit to being defective in

the very sense which should have been more
highly developed in me than in other men, a sense
which I once possessed in its most perfect form, a
form as perfect as few in my profession, surely,
know or have known in the past . . . Recreation in
human society, refined conversation, mutual
effusions of thought are denied to me. Almost quite
alone, I may commit myself to social life only as
far as the most urgent needs demand . . . I might
easily have put an end to my life. Only one thing,
Art, held me back. Oh, it seemed to me impossible
to leave this world before I had produced all that
I felt capable of producing.

This and other quotations from Beethoven, his biographers and his critics are drawn from Charles Waterman's
(Charles Davy's) magnificent and deeply researched study
written for the bicentenary of Beethoven's birth in 1970.*
Charles Davy describes Beethoven as living in two worlds.
He lived in the world of his music, his ideals, and his
reading among great writers; and he lived in the way possible for him in the world of Vienna society, of patrons,
publishers, relatives and friends. The apparent discrepancy
between his behaviour in these two worlds could hardly
have appeared greater. Philip Toynbee summed up the
picture of Beethoven's personal behaviour as given by
Thayer in his three-volume biography: 'Egotistical, arro-
gant, hypochondriacal, self-righteous, dishonest and
malicious'. These words were chosen with the intention of
being quite objective, without adverse judgment. There is
little doubt that Beethoven would have been a 'difficult'
man even if he had not suffered from deafness; and yet his
deafness enhanced all these qualities. It increased his
feeling of grievance against nearly everyone. He wrote in

* *The Golden Blade 1970*, pp. 109–130.

his diary in 1814 'Never show to men the contempt they deserve; one never knows to what use one may want to put them'. He had an overwhelming longing for affectionate relationships. 'Love alone — yes, only love can possibly give me a happier life — O God, let me finally find the one — who will strengthen me in virtue — who will *lawfully* be mine' (1817). Most tragically, this need to love and to be loved was expressed in his relationship to his nephew, Karl. After the death of Karl's father, Beethoven insisted on becoming the sole guardian of the nine-year-old boy and on isolating him from his mother. He treated the boy with alternating overwhelming, possessive affection and uncompromising severity. After about ten years of this treatment Karl was driven to attempted suicide, shooting himself in the head. This is the outstanding example of what Charles Waterman calls 'his almost total incapacity for entering into the feelings of other people and seeing things from their point of view'. He ended the Ninth Symphony with words from Schiller's 'Ode to Joy', expressing boundless love for humanity: 'Be embraced, O ye millions'. But Charles Waterman comments that he himself did not show much inclination to embrace humanity.

And yet he did. Much of the music of the 'second period' of his work expresses his defiant individualism, his angers and desires and above all his intense love of freedom; and this has brought comfort quite literally to millions, and particularly those suffering from loneliness. And this is a fundamental paradox of human nature. It is in the depths of the individual soul, struggling with loneliness that experiences of the most universal kind are to be found. Beethoven expressed this himself; he is reported as saying in 1823, to a visitor:

> You may ask me where I obtain my ideas. I cannot
> answer this with any certainty: they come

unevoked, spontaneously or unspontaneously; I
could grasp them with my hands in the open air,
in the woods, while walking, in the stillness of the
night, at early morning, stimulated by those
moods which the poets turn into words, with me
into tones, which resound, roar and rage until at
last they stand before me in the form of notes.

Beethoven himself was deeply aware of the kinship
between universality and the experience of solitude. He
kept on his desk a copy in his own handwriting, of a
sentence taken from the temple of the goddess Neit at Sais
in Lower Egypt: *He is of himself alone, and it is to this aloneness
that all things owe their being.*

From this mood there gradually developed in him a sense
of peace:

Happy in the woods — every tree has a voice —
through thee, O God, what glory . . . in the hills
is rest — peace to serve Thee.

This was written as early as 1812. The third period of
Beethoven's music is regarded as extending over the last
twelve years of his life, up to his death in 1827. Of the
music of this last period Charles Waterman wrote:

I will say only that it has been taken to suggest a
realisation that the affirmations of the second
period pass over some of the realities of the human
situation, and a searching beyond them for an
acceptance which would be free from self-pity and
from defiance.

Surely it is one of the miracles of human history that a
profoundly lonely, intensely angry and individualistic man
could write music which expresses through centuries for
countless human souls an acceptance of life 'free from self-
pity and from defiance'.

A deaf person might reasonably raise the objection 'You
may tell an artist that his work will be appreciated in the

future — but what comfort is there for me in that, not being an artist?' In reality there is much more creative power in each one of us than we believe. And whether we are deaf, growing deaf, or have good hearing, we can make a beginning with more intensive listening. Sounds do not depend on the ears alone. We can be grateful for what the angel brings to us on whatever path. He is not interested only in helping us to hear, but also in hearing us. He turns his attention to every word, and even to a cry. He feels not only the way in which a word is spoken, its characteristic vowels and consonants, but also its appropriateness. Words have their biographies through the centuries, are born, change, and die. They are in harmony with the moment in which they are spoken, or perhaps grievously disharmonious. They can be too conventional, repeating what everyone is saying, or too egotistical, not really reaching anyone's heart. To all this the angel is very sensitive; and we can hope to listen a little with him. We can look back on a conversation of any kind, and ask how genuine a meeting it contained.

'When two or three are gathered in my name, there I am with them.' The name of Christ need not be mentioned; the intention with which the two or three are met can bring a fulfilment of this promise. A lonely person can come to value such meetings more and more. It is no accident that the numbers two and three are used; he may be able to cope better with such a meeting than with a crowd, especially if he is deaf or old or ill. (A patient in hospital may feel far from happy about a visit by four or more people at once.)

Circumstances often make good encounters difficult and conversations embarrassing, even a move from the north to the south of England or the other way round, in which markedly different accents may be involved. A husband or a wife may feel very lonely in a new environment because of this, or even slighter differences. It is good to regard listening as an adventure, with its joys and dangers. It is reported that Socrates said 'Let me hear his voice that I may know him'. What voices may we not hear tomorrow? Even if a voice is transmitted by telephone or television, with all they do to deprive it of its full character, voices can achieve wonders.

The mood and the intention with which something is said are very often more important than the thoughts that are expressed. Indeed, we cause each other a lot of trouble with our thoughts. Everyone thinks differently; and most of us are rather more interested in our own thoughts than in those of the other person we are talking with. Every effort we make to understand and to respect the thoughts of another brings us nearer to Christ himself in his present reality.

In the ring of the senses, the 'I'-sense and the sense of touch are neighbours; but they are also polar to one another. Through the awareness of the living, conscious 'I' of another we grow far beyond ourselves; through the sense of touch we are aware within our own skin, by the impact made upon us, of something external. When one human being touches another very egotistical emotions can be expressed, for instance anger or desire. The touch may convey a great deal of confirmation and reassurance about the other's acceptability, and justification for existence. We need that everyone who has dealings with us recognizes us as an individual, and some at least hold us dear. From childhood onwards, people vary very much in their willingness to touch, or be touched; an untouchable mother or father can do lasting harm, or a parent may be able to heal considerable pain or shocks. It is not for nothing that many traditional Confirmation services, when the child is passing from childhood to youth, include the laying on of hands.

In this realm much courage and confidence are needed — and also much patience with one another's idiosyncracies. With all five senses that we have now been considering it is very easy to ignore or despise each other's difficulties and threatening loneliness. We know clearly enough when someone is blind; but it is very often said 'So and so can hear well enough when he wants to'. But the beginning of a reluctance to see another 'I' or to be seen oneself may very easily escape notice.

We can and should help each other through dark valleys of loneliness; but we can also know, for ourselves and for others, that these lead to greater companionships and greater creativity in the end, far beyond the limits of this earthly life.

3. The family

When we come to regard the journey of the human soul as alternating between lives on earth and periods in the spiritual world, we can also come to understand and accept quite naturally that the lives on earth are sometimes in a masculine and sometimes in a feminine body. For in most civilizations which we can survey historically the experience of life as a man or as a woman has been markedly different. But generalizations about this difference are threatened by many pitfalls. On the whole it may be said that life as a woman has brought more suffering, life as a man more opportunities for action in a wide sense, particularly the more violent kinds of action. It is possible, too, to call in the conception of the four elements which was touched upon in the last chapter. We may see man's body as more akin to the solid element, and woman's body to the more mobile elements, water, air and fire. This corresponds in a general way to the occupations traditionally undertaken by men — for example, mining, building, ploughing, hunting, and fighting, in which hard tools or weapons are often used, while women have been expected above all to prepare food, with the help of water, air and fire as is done in a most beautiful and complete way in baking bread.

The greatest remedy for loneliness, among grown people, has been found in an enduring love between a man and a woman. And this love is very much influenced by such differences in their bodily natures. Living in a harder body does not necessarily mean that the soul in its entirety becomes harder; but it does usually mean that man's *thinking* is harder and less mobile than a woman's. Masculine thinking is fitted to deal with measurable facts; a woman's may be better in dealing with changing relationships between people which are so full of contradictions. This may make communication between husband and wife very difficult, and turn marriage not into a community but an exceedingly lonely place. The different thoughts, without meeting each other, bring about strong feelings, and iron habits of action. The great joy in each other's different qualities which may have been present at the beginning turns into bitter disappointment.

Of course in actual life there is an infinite variety in the relationships between men and women. And a woman may have a very hard soul life, a man a very gentle one, and yet give each other much happiness and mutual support. It is a question for both of knowing a great deal about themselves and each other and accepting that much cannot be changed quickly — above all, cannot be compelled to change. The better the mutual understanding achieved the better the prospects for a family. But here there is the possibility of very strong disagreements. A woman may want children, a man may veto the idea.

According to descriptions given by Rudolf Steiner, the soul, while still in the spiritual world, comes to know its future mother and father. From the aspect it then has, their difference has a deeply satisfying quality. The mother promises certain qualities of soul which can be shared, the father helps in becoming a strong individuality. The soul helps to achieve its purposes for earth, with the support that mother and father can give both through inheritable qualities and their companionship through childhood and afterwards. But it may have the rude shock of being rejected at the last. Rudolf Steiner himself said very little about abortion. But the veils between the living and the unborn are growing thin. While many women seem able to go through several abortions without thinking or feeling much about them, others are later deeply troubled. A woman who wanted to tell a priest something was unable to say it until he tried to help her by saying: 'Even if you have committed a murder, let us talk about it quietly'. She answered 'That is exactly what I have done'. Most members of her immediate environment, if they had known about her action, would not have regarded it as she now did. We need at the present time the new initiates, some of them women, who from an insight into spirit worlds can tell us about the full social and spiritual consequences of what is happening. It seems as if the rejected soul, though suffering grief, may be able to forgive the parents, even to the extent of coming to them as their child later on. It may then of course find that there are still elements of conflict between mother and father.

Though a good marriage provides the best shelter for children growing up, practically every marriage contains moments of tension. Children can stand, and perhaps even enjoy, a certain amount of conflict in the family, within limits. They can enjoy fighting each other from very early in their lives. But a real break-down of communication between father and mother may bring lastingly harmful consequences. Sometimes one child, generally a daughter, is called upon to arbitrate or to become the recipient of criticisms which are no longer spoken out directly. A woman may suffer throughout her life through having taken on in this way a premature responsibility. She has had to attempt, much too early, to put herself into her father's place and into her mother's place, trying not to give total allegiance to either, at a time when her own relationship to both may present difficulties enough. Sometimes a mother is able to unite children in hostile criticism of their father; probably more seldom a father can do this against the mother.

41

It benefits a family very much if at least one of the parents sees deeply the worthlessness of most criticism. There has never been a time when human beings were so strongly inclined to criticize one another as they are today; and in general, the closer we are to each other, the more we criticize. Both in criticizing, and feeling exposed to criticism, human beings tend to withdraw into themselves. A marriage or any close relationship needs to be able to breathe, to have space; it needs open skies, clear streams, hills and the sea. A deep breath can often show how brittle and arbitrary many criticisms are. They always imply some standard into which the other fails to fit. But what right have we to fabricate and apply such standards to each other? Again and again we have to go back to the fundamental fact; the other is as she is, as he is. All love worthy of the name must start from this. Countless human beings do achieve it, as a matter of course.

A wonderful source for the understanding of the diversities of love and conflict, and of the mysteries of the family, can be found in the plays of Shakespeare. He was himself both a very sociable man, member of a closely-knit family, and extremely lonely. In his early twenties he left his wife and small children at Stratford, to work in London and wandered round England, for much of the year. He came to know people of every class, listening attentively to their vocabulary and manner of speech. As an actor, he had a low place in the class structure of the time; as a man, his modesty and friendliness made him acceptable in every circle. But he felt himself naturally at least as belonging among the counsellors of kings and the bearers of great responsibility; and this discrepancy was painful to him. So much we can gather from the scanty evidence. The best and indeed almost the only source for what Shakespeare felt about himself is in the Sonnets. One of these (No. 29) expresses very powerfully the mood of loneliness among people. It is addressed at the end to the gifted and beautiful young nobleman who was his devoted, though sometimes difficult, friend. (According to some of the best critics this was William Herbert, Earl of Pembroke, nephew of Sir Philip Sidney. William Herbert was later described by the historian Clarendon in a way that remarkably accords with Shakespeare's picture of him in the Sonnets.)

> When, in disgrace with fortune and men's eyes,
> I all alone beweep my outcast state,
> And trouble deaf heaven with my bootless cries,
> And look upon thyself and curse my fate,
> Wishing me like to one more rich in hope,
> Featured like him, like him with friends possess'
> Desiring this man's art, and that man's scope,
> With what I most enjoy contented least;
> Yet in these thoughts myself almost despising,
> Haply I think on thee, and then my state,
> Like to the lark at break of day arising
> From sullen earth, sings hymns at heaven's gate:
> For thy sweet love rememb'red such wealth brings
> That when I scorn to change my state with kings.

Heaven, which was deaf, when he was self-absorbed, or looking at others with jealous eyes, opens and listens at the end. Shakespeare's relationships to the Dark Lady, to whom most of the Sonnets from No. 127 onwards are addressed, seems to have worked differently.

The characters in Shakespeare's plays are not just thought out, the expression of ideas and principles, but are living people, with all the complexity of reality. He is just as good or better as a source of wise information as the reports of sociologists; audiences of many countries, with very different ideologies, feel in his plays the taste of truth. He was very much concerned with fathers and daughters. He saw how decisively the life of a daughter can be influenced by the way in which her father finds or is unable to find his right place in life, his upright bearing among men. It is not always seen how disastrous it is for Ophelia that she relies upon, and obeys, a father who is not upright. It is of great significance for a family that a genuine honesty of purpose *in the world* should shine out from the father. It means much for the daughters of Oedipus that after all the endless trouble of his life, he should win such dignity at the end. It is very hard for a daughter if she cannot help regarding her father as through and through a failure, or as having deserted her (even by dying) when she needed him. For her own healthy sense of individuality, she needs to respect him, to be able to help or even heal him (as Marina does in *Pericles*) and be independent of him — all at the same time.

If this many-tinted relationship is not there in a woman's life, or is broken at a crucial moment, a deep sense of loneliness is likely to follow, which may show itself in a quite drastic kind of withdrawal. If she marries, she may look for the missing father in her husband, and he may again disappoint her. Great willingness to face the truth, on both sides, may here be necessary.

Twentieth-century ideas about *sons* and fathers have been haunted by a one-sided conception of the destiny of Oedipus. Shakespeare had a wider horizon than Freud. The relationship between father and son is perhaps most wonderfully described in *Henry IV*, (II, IV, V). While the aged and troubled Henry IV is at last sleeping, his son tentatively tries on his crown. His father catches him at it and reproaches him bitterly. In his son's answer there is a wonderful mingling of respect and independence. Henry IV's criticism of his son is devastating. Young Henry, he says, is only longing for the moment when his father is laid into the grave, and he can take power, which he will use to let loose every kind of violence and lawlessness.

44

O my poor kingdom! thick with civil blows —
When that my care could not withhold thy riots,
What wilt thou do when riot is thy care?
O! thou wilt be a wilderness again,
Peopled with wolves, thy old inhabitants.

The Prince answers gently that he does not desire his
father's death, or to have power himself; his crown,
although it is the image of the authority of God, has
been his father's enemy, bringing an intolerable burden of
care — and will be his own. In this picture very much is
said about the relationship of fathers and sons. The son
expects to find in the father, not only upright dealing in
general, but a capacity to carry responsibility as something
entrusted to him by the spiritual world. But every man is
unworthy in some way of the responsibility given to him;
and on earth this wears him out. The son longs to achieve
the same degree of responsibility, but will in turn be
weighed down by it. Thus there is in the young Henry,
together with the genuine respect for his father and the
determination to take his future responsibility with the
greatest seriousness, a note of compassion both for his
father and for himself — though not in the sense of self-
pity.

In the present too, fathers often criticize their sons. But
they have much less confidence about their right to do so;
while the sons have little doubt about their right and need
to criticize their fathers. Very often it is because they see
in their father a basic weakness, a kind of abdication of
responsibility — though this is compatible with violent
resentment about any attempt by the father to dominate.

Not only in childhood but right on into later life, sons
and daughters look to their mother to keep the family
together, to some extent at least, and perhaps even to have
room for them in her house when they want it. Shakespeare
seems to have been much less concerned with the relation-

ship between daughters and mothers, though it is a region by no means free of drama. Daughters are often, individually, quite devastatingly critical of their mothers, from adolescence for the next twenty years or so; while their help may be very necessary, everything about them is wrong, including their choice of clothes, their cooking, and their political views. One daughter on a shopping expedition complained first of her mother talking too loudly, then that she spoke in whispers, and then asked why she did not talk at all. 'Mother, are you dumb?'

Such tensions need not be regarded as simply negative; sometimes they are part of a necessary path to independence. The mother may try too much to mould the daughter; and she may even, if the father withdraws in some way, take on what used to be regarded as his role so thoroughly that she becomes something of a tyrant. And then those of the family who cannot stand this may simply escape — and perhaps become lonely.

Up to this point the family has been spoken of as if it contained at least two or three children. But of course the general tendency, over much of the world, is for the family to decrease in size until families with more than two children become rare exceptions. The effect of this is that everyone will have fewer and fewer relatives of any sort, including cousins and second cousins, and that the likelihood of tension and loneliness within and around the nuclear family becomes even greater. The tendency goes further still; there are many families, and there will be more, where there is only one active parent. This may be a temporary condition, as at times when a father is called away by his work to another region or country; probably millions of African families are deprived for long periods of a father who works in distant towns or mines. The mother then often takes on the full burden of children and smallholding; and both parents are lonely.

Then we should remember homosexual couples (who are seldom in a position to adopt children, were they to wish to do so). Many people in these categories are exposed, though of course in very different ways, to criticisms of a kind that may make them very lonely. People in their environment may not even attempt to understand them in any depth. It is good if they try to do this themselves, though not at all easy. Even an almost unendurable situation is only transitory and something positive begins to grow within it. The soul can look at other times of its existence, within or beyond this earthly incarnation. The angels, if they are consulted, are able to give help.

As a first step in this process, many individual souls are coming to feel questions about their earthly incarnations as more and more pressing. 'Why did I come to these parents? To this place on earth? At this time in history? I do not belong here!' More and more souls feel, even in early childhood, and increasingly up to their early twenties, that they had some kind of existence before they put on this earthly body — perhaps long before they encounter this idea in the writings of Plato, or Rudolf Steiner, or in other books. This feeling may be hard to bring to full consciousness or to express in clear words. Shakespeare, in *Twelfth Night*, lets the noble Sebastian, appearing as if reborn from the sea, put it very exactly:

A spirit I am indeed;
But am in that dimension grossly clad
Which from the womb I did participate.

What was experience in the spiritual world before birth gradually seeks to renew itself. Shakespeare in his plays often makes a clear distinction between the serious-minded, though by no means humourless, people who have this feeling, and the more frivolous ones who do not (in *Twelfth*

47

Night, Sir Toby Belch and his companions). Before birth the soul participated in the great, solemn, creative cosmic Word, resounding through all being. And as the child grows up, it longs to regain some of its universality, perhaps by learning new languages and becoming absorbed in different cultures.

Rudolf Steiner has indicated that it will gradually become possible for human beings looking attentively at their lives to find the significance of seven-year periods — from birth to seven, from seven to fourteen, from fourteen to twenty-one, and so on. For example, a strong emotional experience in one such period will find its developing consequences at some point in each subsequent period. The impulses which lead to separation and solitude may thus work afresh at about nine years old, at sixteen, and onwards through life — not necessarily at seven-year intervals precisely, but within each seven-year period. Thus within the pattern of a human life we have natural rhythms, but also the sudden events, like those described in the last chapter, which at first run counter to the natural development but are then absorbed into its flow like ripples from a stone thrown into a stream.

Thus the development of the family is complex indeed; its members come at different times to their moments of withdrawal, and to the seventh anniversaries of turning-points in their lives. Always it is under stress; but this need not weary or weaken its members, if they can grow increasingly interested in one another. And this will apply in the future more and more to other kinds of community, not linked by ties of blood, but by shared constructive purposes.

Particularly from the age of twenty-one onwards, human beings seek something like a new family, not related by blood. The new languages it seeks out then, or sometimes much later, can be a tremendous help in this. Each new language we learn, and to some extent make our own, develops something like a new part of our invisible being. A learned Japanese writer, Professor Tadahiro Ohnuma, has described this process very beautifully. He began, on a visit to Britain, to get inside English, though he had learned it in an external sense much earlier:

> I became acutely sensitive towards English
> pronunciation, stress, rhythm and intonation, and
> moreover I sensed that a subtle body had started
> to become active within me — a subtle body which
> could vibrate very energetically and which was
> differently formed from the subtle body which I,
> as a Japanese, possessed. It was not so much that
> my sense of self had *split*, but rather that a second
> self had been born within me. Like an alchemist I
> carefully reared this homunculus inside me until,
> after a month's hard training he could feel, think
> and speak in English. On my behalf he produced
> most naturally a way of thinking and an attitude
> one associated with the English language and
> which no Japanese would normally think of.

Through speaking or singing words in another language the sensitivity and delicacy of our hearing and speech sense, briefly described in the last chapter, are enhanced. The formation of the new family is very much aided by deep-going conversation, in which both partners really listen to each other, and the thought sense and 'I'-sense are also stirred to activity. Small groups may be formed in this way whose members may feel themselves called to share tasks which will last for the rest of their lives. And sometimes they may feel quite confidently 'We have been together in earlier lives — perhaps working together as we do now, or perhaps as opponents'. And perhaps within such a group, some of them find their future husbands or wives.

All this contributes to the formation of new relationships

with the original family given by birth. The feeling for father, mother, sisters and brothers can now change into a steady friendship, with mutual respect for the freedom of the other. It may be necessary about this time to accept and use a new name instead of the one given at birth, however wisely and lovingly. It has long been the well-considered practice of orders of monks or nuns to use new names for the ones who have taken their vows and are addressed as Brother or Sister. In the Eastern Orthodox Church there is an opportunity to change names even earlier in life, at Confirmation.

Soon after Confirmation, and increasingly after the age of twenty-one, the need to pray and meditate develops. These things can be done in groups or in solitude. Periods of loneliness provide special opportunities for them. Into spaces that have begun to ache with emptiness divine powers enter who can be listened to, and who listen.

Both the original family and the new family can become wider in this way; and they can be joined as well by those who have belonged to them and have died. In Japan, of course no family is regarded as complete, without the spirits of its ancestors; and someone from another country who had married into a Japanese family might seek out the house where the spirits of a husband's or wife's ancestors were particularly honoured at times when difficult decisions had to be reached.

The relationships between children and their grandparents often contain much less emotional stress than those to their parents. And after the death of the grandparents we may look back, perhaps for the rest of our lives, with a certain tranquil gratitude. The relationship to great-grandparents and those still further back, are even less likely to be very emotional — perhaps consisting mainly in the knowledge of a few facts and anecdotes about them. But the death of a parent is something like an earthquake, and a quiet and positive mood about it may not be achieved for many years. Yet by far the worst kind of bereavement is where a husband or a wife dies after years of a good marriage, leaving a widow or widower. Our civilization is not very helpful about this. It is inclined to admire a widow if she seems after a few months to have recovered from her grief and be living a fully active normal life. But it may be just at this time that the loss of the physical presence of husband or wife is felt most deeply. Conscientious research has shown that deaths from heart disease are much higher among widowers than men of other categories. A good relationship with the one who has died is hindered, if the soul on earth lacks tranquillity.

I knew a woman who had made an agreement with her husband that when one of them died, he or she would give the surviving partner convincing evidence of survival. The husband died first and the widow was always looking for external evidence of his presence. This made her life much more restless and troubled than it need have been. It was impossible to convince her that she was not looking in the right direction for tokens of his continued care for her.

These tokens are to be found deep within us or in small incidents that we may easily ignore. They are to be observed not by the head but by the heart and other organs of the body. They may come in gentle warnings, as if it were being whispered to us: 'You do not know all the results that may follow from the action you have in mind. Perhaps you can hold back your words and actions until you are more peaceful'.

Rudolf Steiner gave indications in abundance about the experience of the soul and how a good relationship between the living and the dead can be cultivated. We do not keep for ever the language we have spoken on earth; indeed, the word-sense, thought-sense and 'I'-sense all drop away from us. This makes many apparent communications through some kind of automatic writing unsatisfactory. The soul is learning a new heavenly language and would like us to share a little in this. It is a great help if we can cultivate certain moods of soul, which reach far beyond the domain of earthly language.

Firstly, we can strengthen our realization that we are intimately involved with the people and events in the world around us. Well before middle life, we have been influenced by people in many countries of the earth; and the effects of our own words and actions have flowed out, far beyond the limits of our own knowledge. We have contributed to the happiness or unhappiness of people who are now on the other side of the earth. Of such things the dead are aware; and it is in a sense a puzzle for them that we on earth regard ourselves so much as detached objects, things in themselves. We come to meet them by remembering our community with all creatures.

Secondly — though we may well choose to work at this mood first of all — we need to grow in thankfulness. We have received far more good than evil from life. Thankfulness can extend to such things as the air we breathe and the light we see, which are generally taken for granted. This mood provides a strong bridge of positive feelings over into the world of the dead. When we remember thankfully someone we have known who has died we give them something that resembles the joy we can feel on earth through music or beautiful works of art.

The third mood is the most difficult for people on earth at the present time to develop in a steady way. It is confidence in the future. We do not know what is going to happen in our own lives, we do not know what is going to happen on the earth. Nagging anxiety is difficult to avoid. We need the conviction that good powers have foreseen the dangers threatening us personally and threatening the world. They, and the dead with them, see through present darknesses to coming steady light. They see that without the darkness the light later on would not develop as it should. And if we in our conscious mind have not enough grasp of this there is a barrier between us and the worlds of spirit. The barrier can only be converted into a bridge through a strong belief in the invisible. All life that is destroyed continues in another form. William Blake had unshakable confidence in this respect. In his poem 'Night', he describes sheep attacked by wolves:

And if they rush dreadful
The Angels, most heedful,
Receive each mild spirit
New worlds to inherit.

Modern feelings may reject such words as sentimental — but Blake meant them completely as a description of fact, even if it was a fact that only innocent eyes could see. Children have faith in the future; they should not be compelled to lose it.

For the fourth mood it is difficult to find a single, comprehensive word. It is the very opposite of the feeling expressed in the saying: 'There is nothing new under the sun'. Every morning it is possible to hope for much in the coming day that will bring unforeseen joy. To look at things and people as if we had never seen them before, and delight in them, this preserves an inner youthfulness all through life. Rudolf Steiner is described as having something of an argument with a person near to him about a third person, to whom he wanted to entrust a considerable responsibility. 'But you spoke about him very critically yesterday!' 'Yes, that was yesterday.' We are cumbered with static thoughts about other people, which it is too much effort to move and this is very troublesome for the dead. They live in worlds of wonderful, manifest change. And though they want to be remembered, they do not want us only to hold in our minds pictures and thoughts about them exactly as

they were at the end of their earthly lives. Particularly
when death came in unforeseen and grievous ways we can
become obsessed and imprisoned by what happened. But
the soul has left this behind, and has changed. A child who
has died can be pictured as grown older, quite soon; an
old person has grown younger. The auras of both now
manifest different colours, maybe with wings. The traces
of illnesses or disabilities they have had do not disappear
at once, but in the course of time — though the experience
of time on the other side is rather different — are marvel-
lously transformed. A disabled person may have foretastes
of this in his dreams. The worst thing for the dead is when
grievances and bitter criticisms continue to be held against
them. (Earlier civilizations understood this much better
than we do.) It is for the dead as if they had to struggle
through brambles. They need to be forgiven, and seen as
having potentialities they did not develop on earth.

Our growth in these four moods will of course not be
enough in itself to enable us to have fully conscious conversations with those who have died. But a special warmth,
and an enlivening of our thinking, will flow into us, and
support us in what we have to do. On the other hand, a
grief may sometimes invade us, the source of which we
cannot at first identify. And this may be from someone
who has died, who has difficulties in reconciling herself or
himself with the unaccustomed conditions in the spiritual
world — perhaps someone of whose death we have not yet
heard, and who may still want to look at the physical world
through our eyes — not wrongly, but in a way that will
change.

The support that can be received from the dead need
not be thought of as coming from this person or that person
separately, but will often be from souls working together.
A human being approaching death may meet souls dear
to him or her who have died before. Their powers can unite

to warm and illumine people still on earth — particularly those who have gone before us, as is rightly felt in many communities. That this grows stronger in the world, whether the communities concerned call themselves Christian or not, is intimately related to the work of the Christ.

4. The solitude of God and men

For the last two or three centuries there has been an ever-developing interest in ancient civilizations, both through what can be learned about them from archaeology and through traditions and customs still alive, particularly among peoples to some extent protected from the onrush of change. In general it seems that we are led back into forms of human consciousness in which groups of people felt deeply united, and not as separate, individually responsible selves. There is much evidence that the experience of 'we' is older and stronger, in early times, than the experience of 'I'. Families, tribes and races joyed and sorrowed together, and made decisions together, like migrating birds. But there were always individuals who stood out, making their own decisions, taking special responsibilities. And while in general the group suffered bereavement as a whole, particularly at the death of such great ones, the great ones themselves could suffer bereavement in a solitary way.

From the Greek civilization we have inherited for such people the name 'hero'. The basic meaning of this word is said to be 'protector', like the name of the goddess Hera. In times of stress or danger the hero was felt as protecting his people. But his power to guard and to help was bought at a price. He or she could suffer and be lonely in ways that others could not.

The great Greek tragedies illustrate this very clearly. The chorus feels its joys and sorrows as a group; it can forget or contradict itself without any sense of inconsistency. The two or three protagonists are right out in front, exposed and alone. We might say that every member of the chorus is extremely thankful not to be a hero. For heroes and heroines have such appalling troubles. The chorus fails to comfort them; but generally each hero or heroine has a god or goddess who can and does bring help. And this is a striking thing: the gods have sympathy for the lonely struggles of men. Sometimes indeed the hero is himself partly a god, or the offspring of a god. But how is it that the gods have compassion for loneliness and bereavement? Are they not part of an immortal company, beyond the reach of pain? Evidently for the Greeks this is not altogether so: there are partings and sorrows among the immortals as well.

We can look further back to a civilization which the Greeks themselves regarded as much older than theirs. Osiris is a god (though not one of the very oldest, it seems). He lives on earth as a gifted and inventive king, bringing peace and progress both to his own and to neighbouring peoples. Agriculture in particular makes great advances. But he is treacherously killed by his brother, and has to live afterwards in the underworld, to which the souls of men come after death. His wife Isis, though herself divine, endlessly suffers, and seeks for what is left of his body. She has an ally, in her conflict with the murderer of her husband, her son Horus; but all those who rightly seek for heavenly wisdom become her sons. Her noble grief and her power to protect are united in her as one deep element of her being.

The Greeks have themselves a goddess who suffers the loss of one dear to her. The earth-goddess Demeter is in some way alone among the immortals from the beginning. But her love for her daughter, Persephone, is complete and without end. And when Persephone is stolen by Pluto, the god of the underworld, she looks for her everywhere, overcome with grief. At first no-one in heaven or on earth will tell her where Persephone is, whether out of ignorance, or fearing to tell her the truth. And when she learns of Pluto's deed she cannot at first counter it herself. It is Hermes, the divine messenger, who can bring about the agreement that Persephone shall live part of the year on earth and part still in Hades. The meeting of mother and daughter is filled with joy; but sorrow remains part of Demeter's nature, and she is more isolated than before among the gods, particularly because she feels that Zeus has conspired with Pluto. Like Isis, she inspires the pupils of the mysteries, especially those who are to become pioneers in agriculture. Isis and Demeter endure bereavement because of the deeds of other gods, representative of dark worlds.

Almost at the beginning of the Hebrew story of mankind a loneliness is described which originates in a man's own guilt. This is preceded by two stories of creation; one going through six world-days, culminating when the archetype of man is formed which transcends the difference between man and woman, and is directly the image of God. Later Adam is formed out of earth: he is incomplete and seeks companionship. Eve is created to fulfil his need. After their Fall, their sons take up different tasks on earth. Cain tills the ground, Abel is a shepherd. And while God accepts the offerings of Abel, he rejects those of Cain. In jealousy Cain kills Abel. After this deed Cain has to live long on earth, a wanderer and outcast, though his descendants become pioneers in crafts and the life of cities generally. Nothing seems to make good his act, nothing seems to bring him back into the communities of heaven and of earth. He meets everywhere the knowledge that he is the murderer of the brother he has lost.

In the Babylonian tradition there is again a man who wanders through many lands in deep loneliness, though a very different destiny from that of Cain has brought him to this. Gilgamesh ventures to oppose Ishtar, the goddess of love. And as a consequence Ishtar brings about an epidemic in which the friend and heroic companion he has found dies. Gilgamesh has a great sorrow no-one can share. And his journey has the motive of finding at last the answer to the mystery of death. In Europe he becomes the pupil of a great priest of the mysteries, but he cannot completely achieve the tasks which are set him. He returns to his own city with his deepest questions unanswered.

When we meet such figures in the holy books and great epics of antiquity, they are to be regarded both as real individualities and as representatives of countless others, who are to tread similar destinies in later times. More and more people, who may not seem to others particularly oustanding, endure at least in part the sufferings which were the hard privilege of heroes and heroines. Shakespeare's kings would not fascinate us so much if a king was not hidden in everyone. There is a figure in one of the plays of Sophocles, who is neither a king nor quite a hero, and might almost be described as an ordinary man. Philoctetes is a Greek soldier on his way with the others to the siege of Troy, when he inadvertently offends a goddess by treading in a place sacred to her. His punishment is a hard one; his foot is afflicted with a disease which brings him intolerable pain, and which stinks in the nostrils of his companions. They abandon him upon a lonely island. The play begins when Odysseus and a young companion come back from Troy years later to fetch him — because an oracle has revealed that without him Troy cannot be taken. Sophocles here gives a picture of loneliness and its consequences which could hardly be more complete. Philoctetes is in no mood to accept the late and self-seeking repentance of his faithless friends; and an intervention from the realm of the immortals is necessary. Herakles, the hero raised to the heavens after victory in many trials, appears among them, and by his revelation restores brotherhood and mutual trust between Philoctetes and the Greeks.

If we return, across two millennia, to the plays of Shakespeare, we find his loneliest figure not deserted upon an island but constantly among people. Hamlet had been a particularly sociable young man; and he is rendered solitary by no crime or offence of his own, but by the secret murder of his father, and the quick marriage of his mother, the queen, to the murderer. Gertrude is in a similar position to that of Isis, but acts very differently (though there is a hint in Plutarch of a momentary weakness of Isis towards Typhon, for which Horus rebukes her). The intervention by the ghost of Hamlet's father cannot bring any reconciliation, and drives Hamlet deeper into solitude, because he cannot speak of it to anyone, and is even divided within himself about its reality.

The whole play has been described as a meditation on death. There is much in this; but there is another theme which pervades it still more thoroughly. Everywhere we see human speech struggling towards genuine communication, and being defeated. If we observe attentively we find that no-one really understands what anybody else says, sometimes not even the speaker himself. Even when people love each other, as Hamlet loves Ophelia and his friend Horatio, they speak different and mutually incomprehensible languages — 'wild and whirling words'. And they cannot pray either; Claudius is shown trying to pray, but knows that he cannot genuinely repent for the murder he has done. 'The words fly up, the thoughts remain below.' When Hamlet knows that he is dying, he speaks of the ceasing of this tumult of words: 'The rest is silence'. And Horatio responds: 'Goodnight, sweet prince: And flights of angels sing thee to thy rest.' Gentle heavenly voices must be heard before Hamlet's loneliness can be healed. Before writing *Hamlet*, Shakespeare had shown several times on his stage the loneliness of a king or prince; both Richard II and Richard III are examples of this. Richard II is seen in prison struggling desperately with his conflicting thoughts. But the loneliness of Richard III is still more terrible; in his tent at night he is assailed by a whole series of visions of the dead condemning him for his many murders. There seems no hope of reconciliation on any level of existence. Then at the end of Shakespeare's working life, when he returns to the writing of a historical play after many years, he shows Queen Katherine banished from court by the husband she still loves, Henry VIII. She lives in a country place with a few servants. She is still very conscious of her dignity as a queen, but has forgiven Henry and all her enemies. There appear to her shining personages in a solemn dance, inviting her to a great banquet. And we know that this will be after her approaching death.

By Shakespeare's time, the chorus has long disappeared. But in some of the plays there is a background of figures who are shown not so much as responsible individuals, but as representatives of a general mood and this happens to some extent in *Henry VIII*. London crowds appear (or are described) in whom is reflected something of the fortunes and misfortunes of the great ones.

If we look back some fifteen hundred years to the period of early Christian history during which the four Gospels were written we see that crowds of people, called in general 'the multitude', play a great part. Christ speaks to them and they respond with awe, with questions, sometimes with dissent. They feel as a group. The disciples listen with different ears: they have passed through experiences which make them more individual, much more capable of independent thought. A surprisingly large part of what we find as sayings in the Gospels is spoken to the disciples. In St Matthew's Gospel there are five considerable passages, of which the first is the Sermon on the Mount, mainly addressed to the disciples, though their impact is felt by the crowd.

In the first three Gospels very little is spoken directly to individuals: though the Christ is often described as healing particular people of their infirmities. But in all four Gospels we meet at the outset a mighty, solitary individual — John the Baptist. He has left his parents some time before and dwelt in the wilderness, experiencing to the full what it means for a man to live alone. He is a solitary not through guilt, or through rejection by men, but by a vocation received from God. Later he is to endure desperate solitude again, not far from the place of his sojourn in the wilderness, imprisoned in the fortress of Herod by the Dead Sea. But in the interval many come out to him, and receive a baptism which leads towards individual consciousness; and some become his disciples.

There is another category of people who come to John: they are 'scribes and Pharisees', or their representatives. They have left the wide dream-consciousness of the multitude, and grown into a narrowly intellectual understanding of the Law. They are constantly dissatisfied with what they hear. They can only accept what the Spirit revealed long ago, so far as they can understand it, but cannot hear its living voice.

In the Gospel of St John, the Christ is described as coming to 'his own' — as it is usually translated. But the Greek word used here really means individual men, men as bearers of an 'I'. It is in this Gospel that the Christ is most often described as dealing with individual men and women, and as awakening in them faith in him through what he says and does. It is a man who has deeply experienced solitude, and who has achieved a great sense of individual responsibility, from whom Jesus receives baptism. And it is followers of John who become his own first disciples. The very first are Andrew and an un-named

4. THE SOLITUDE OF GOD AND MEN

disciple who come together with Jesus to the place where
he is abiding. And then, Peter, Philip and Nathanael are
found separately, and in particular ways. (The other
Gospels describe the calling of the disciples differently, and
at a later stage: the accounts need not be regarded as
contradictory, but as recording diverse occasions.) And
then scattered through the Gospel we have people with
whom Jesus speaks, people in very varied situations, but
most of whom have in common that they are in some way
cut off from their fellow-men, or have taken a notable
personal decision. Nicodemus comes to Jesus by night,
alone. The Samaritan woman comes alone at midday to
Jacob's well. The man who has suffered for thirty-eight
years from paralysis complains that he has no-one to help
him. The man born blind is isolated by his disability and
as a beggar. The woman taken in adultery is in the terrible
solitude of one condemned by everyone. And to each, Jesus
responds in a way that meets this special destiny. In the
conversation with the Samaritan woman we can observe
how the dialogue advances step by step from the quite
general request for water to drink, to the woman's deep
question about the coming of the Messiah, and Christ's
declaration of who he is. The woman understands that the
one with whom she speaks knows already the story of her
life. What has been described in this book as a sense
possessed by men in general, the 'I'-sense, Jesus has on a
different level: the complete vision of a human being's
individuality and development. Thus recognized and
accepted, she who came in unhappy solitude could go back
without hesitation to her city and bring others to Jesus.

The story of the man born blind is much more remarkable than is generally noticed. To begin with it is taken for
granted that blindness must be the result of 'sin'. 'Who
sinned, this man or his parents, that he was born blind?'
Only in a previous life could this man himself have sinned,

if it was his own act that brought blindness upon him. Those who thought in this way had looked at the blind man throughout his life with condemnation in their eyes. And even those who regarded his parents as responsible thought of the man as blameworthy too: 'You were born in utter sin.' But Jesus says, 'It was not that this man sinned, or his parents, but that the works of the God might be made minifest in him.' This manifestation is plainly not only the healing itself, but in the whole sequence of events; the endurance of the disability, the healing, in which the man plays an active part himself, and his subsequent deeds of witness, in which he shows notable courage. He is willing to become an outcast now in a different way, for the sake of the truth.

The story is a mysterious and complex preparation for the account of the raising of Lazarus, also told only in St John's Gospel. The very first thing that is said about Lazarus is that he was sick. But he is loved by Jesus. From the point of view of all four Gospels, this is a tremendous paradox. Jesus gives health to everyone who needs his help. No-one dies, or comes near death, in his presence. How could a close disciple, loved by him, fall sick? Has he then committed some great sin, which separates him from his master? Nothing in the story suggests this. And what is said by Jesus about the sickness is directed towards the future, like his words about the blind man. The sickness is not unto death, but for the manifestation of God. It is always possible to look at human illnesses with the question 'For what is this a preparation?' A situation may arise in a human destiny where something is being asked of us, which we cannot fulfil. Instead, we may fall ill, or suffer some accident. It may be years before we are faced with a similar challenge; and now we may be able to meet it fully, because of the inner development which the illness or accident has helped to bring about in us. Can the sickness

of Lazarus perhaps be regarded in this light? There is a
further far-reaching question: is Lazarus in any sense a
solitary figure, as many of those with whom Jesus is specially concerned are indicated by the Gospel as being? He is
beloved by Christ, has two devoted sisters, and seems to
be a member of the circle of disciples. How can he be in
any sense lonely?

A man can be very much loved and respected, and look
up to a teacher very much greater than himself — and yet
be alone with a task which the teacher, for good reasons,
will not help him with directly, and about which no one
else can advise. Almost from the beginning, Christ had
indicated to the disciples that he would be put to death by
his enemies. For instance they heard him say, after the
cleansing of the Temple (in words referring, as St John
specifically says, to his own body): 'Destroy this Temple
and I will build it up again after three days.' All the
Gospels show that the disciples were not able to come to
terms with such words. In his account of the Transfiguration, Luke shows with whom understanding for the
approaching Passion could be found; Jesus speaks on the
mountain with the spiritual forms of Moses and Elijah
'about his Exodus which he would accomplish in Jerusalem'. It is evident that the three disciples who were
present could not comprehend what was being said.
Months later, immediately before his last coming to Jerusalem, Jesus speaks in some detail of the approaching
Passion; and Luke says 'that they understood none of these
things; this saying was hid from them, and they did not
grasp what was said.' Was Lazarus one of those (as his
sister Martha clearly was) who did not understand? In a
delicate way the story indicates that he understood much
more than the others. For he stays in Bethany when the
others have gone with Jesus 'across the Jordan to the place
where John at first baptized'. Bethany is near Jerusalem,

65

on the road which comes from Jericho across the desert, on the slopes of the Mount of Olives. During Holy Week, Jesus comes out at night to Bethany, except on the night before the Passion.

Thus Lazarus prepares in a different way for what is to happen, perhaps only a few weeks later. Jesus has taken the other disciples into the desert country 'beyond Jordan', and there they are reminded of John the Baptist, who had said of Jesus, 'Behold the Lamb of God, who bears the sin of the world.' Lazarus remains near Jerusalem, where the cosmic Offering of the Lamb, prefigured in the Passover before the Exodus, is to be accomplished. Lazarus is thus in a very deep sense alone; he has to ponder, separated in space from Jesus and the other disciples, and near to the enemies of Jesus, what he has to do when the crucial moment, the moment of the Cross, actually comes. His sisters have not come near enough to the mysterious relationship between Christ and death to be able to help him. It is not just a question of being able to understand, when the time comes; he must be able to act, when an event is coming about before him, unlike anything that has happened before on earth. Only one thing will really prepare him; he has himself to die, and be raised from death.

One of the first things to be revealed by Rudolf Steiner, when he began to teach as an initiate about the spiritual world, was that Lazarus is himself the author of the fourth Gospel. In the Gospels names are used in a particular way, which must seem to us unusual. The same person may be referred to by different names at different times according to the situation. For instance, in St John's Gospel itself, although Peter has been given his name by Jesus, he is repeatedly addressed in the last chapter as Simon. In St Luke's Gospel, written as it seems some time before the fourth Gospel, we find the story of Lazarus the beggar, who dies, and for whose resurrection the rich man who neglected him in life pleads with Abraham.

Lazarus of Bethany is a beggar in a different sense. The candidate for initiation into the mysteries of the spiritual world has to pass through severe trials; among them, he has to achieve the recognition that everything he has achieved so far in his search for knowledge is really nothing at all; and he has to see that he cannot yet free his will from its over-attachment to earthly things. In the old mysteries he came, under the influence of such trials, to the point where he could undergo a kind of death. He was laid into a grave, and after three days raised to life again by the chief Hierophant. During this period his life-forces had been detached from his physical body, as they are at the end of ordinary lives, and had dwelt consciously in the spiritual world. Rudolf Steiner shows how what what happens is both like and unlike these ancient procedures. Lazarus too is laid in the grave, and called back after three and a half days by Christ himself, as a transformed being. Through this he becomes capable of writing the fourth Gospel, and refers to himself there as 'the beloved disciple', not out of presumption but with boundless gratitude for what he has received.

One of the far-reaching riddles that arise, when we compare the four Gospels with one another, concerns the events John leaves out. Matthew, Mark and Luke describe the Transfiguration, and give an account of the institution of the holy sacrament: John does not. The others describe how Jesus prays alone in the Garden of Gethsemane. John goes straight from the end of the Last Supper to the arrest of Jesus. It would certainly be wrong to think that John leaves things out *because* they have been related already; for he tells the story of the Feeding of the Five Thousand, which is also told by the other Evangelists. One answer that may be suggested, and may contain at least part of the truth, is that where John leaves something out the *meaning* of that event is spread out through the whole Gospel, or a considerable part of it. For instance, the whole Gospel may be regarded as existing on the same spiritual level as the conversation of Jesus with Moses and Elijah at the Transfiguration, and containing the same essential content.

What is described as the agony of Jesus in the Garden of Gethsemane is a deeply moving and mysterious event. The Trial of Jesus and the Passion are approaching; and Jesus faces their coming in solitary prayer. Even a small chosen group of disciples — the same as at the Transfiguration — is not able to keep awake with him. We are onlookers at a terrible paradox: the loneliness of a god.

Why does John, who knows so much about loneliness, not include this? Perhaps, part of the answer is this; the whole of the Farewell Discourses, and the High-Priestly Prayer (chapters 14–17) are concerned with the same thing, as the accounts of the Last Supper in the other Gospels are not. Matthew, Mark and Luke are chiefly concerned there with the institution of the sacrament which the disciples received with profound reverence and in unity, as in Fra Angelico's wonderful picture. In St John the difficulties that the disciples are having are shown by the questions four of them ask, interrupting the stream of the discourse. Peter, Thomas, Philip, and the other Judas intervene with their personal problems, holding back the great commission that is being given to them all. And Jesus himself describes what is happening just before his great prayer to the Father. 'The hour is coming, indeed it has come, when you will be scattered, every man to his home, and will leave me alone; yet I am not alone, for the Father is with me.'

The translation 'his home' though the usual and indeed natural one for the Greek *ta idia*, is perhaps inappropriate or even mistaken here. There is no other indication that the Galilean disciples had anything like homes in Jerusalem. Literally it means 'the own things' and it is the same word which in the first chapter of John's Gospel is translated 'individual men' by Rudolf Steiner. The disciples are thrown back utterly upon themselves; they pass through the following events like dreamers, completely unable to take any effective action or speak any helpful word. Among earthly men Jesus is left alone. No-one stands by him, to help answer the accusations of his enemies; there is no-one even to share in part of his suffering. Everyone fails to understand what is happening. The darkness over the world is in human souls too. This complete lack of understanding is the Cup which Jesus must accept at Gethsemane. It is a drink which only makes worse the thirst of the soul for understanding, the thirst declared by Jesus on the Cross, in the saying recorded only by John.

But there are nevertheless a few who bring understanding. One of them is 'the disciple whom Jesus loved'; another is his mother. It is not always seen how lonely Mary must have become, after the people of Nazareth had rejected and attempted to stone Jesus. Her other sons, of whom Mark gives a list, did not understand Jesus. But she did, even from the time of the Baptism: she could work with him in his first sign, at Cana in Galilee. But it is clear that she did not ordinarily accompany him on his journeys. There is a very beautiful drawing by Dürer of Jesus saying farewell to his mother; and perhaps there was more than one such farewell. Now, from the Cross, Jesus institutes a new relationship, saying to his mother 'Woman, behold your son!' and to the beloved disciple 'Behold your mother!' In the next sentence we find again the Greek words *ta idia*; the disciple takes her into his individual decisions and responsiblities. There does not seem to be anything to indicate a residence by Mary at Bethany; but she may well

69

have had her home later on at Ephesus, with which the beloved disciple is connected by a definite early tradition.

At the Cross we find in this way a wonderful example of how loneliness prepares for its own healing. Had not both Mary and the beloved disciple gone upon very solitary paths, they would not have been to each other what they now become. Mary brings a deep insight into the mysteries of birth, John the harvest of his encounter with death. They can raise the relationship of mother and son, which has been so powerful in human instincts for millennia, back into the realm of eternal light. And Christ during the hours of his greatest solitude can prepare for individual human beings a new realm of intensive relationships transforming and transcending those of the natural blood, as he himself pours out his blood upon the earth.

5. Resurrection and Ascension

Very little is said in the New Testament about the events which happened between Christ's death upon the Cross on Good Friday and his resurrection early on Easter Sunday. There is a brief reference in the First Letter of Peter, where it is said Christ went and 'preached to the spirits in prison'; and there are some vivid imaginative descriptions in early Christian apocryphal writings which were then developed during the Middle Ages into plays on the theme of the harrowing of hell. The 'spirits in prison' are those who at that time were dwelling in the realms after death but had been so deeply influenced by their experiences in the earthly body that they could not find their way out of the temporal into eternal being. Sub-terrestrial spirits try to hold them under their influence; Christ comes to free them and set their feet on the great ladder towards the stars. As St Paul indicates, Christ does not leave to the dark powers undisputed sway in the depths of the earth. He claims hell as well as earth as his realm entrusted to him by his Father. It is the beginning of a long battle to redeem evil, bringing it back into cosmic harmony. Today, countless souls who have died meet him as Being of Light; remarkable testimony about this has come from a number of people who have been pronounced dead in hospital but have resuscitated. The Being of Light, whom they may prefer not to call by any other name, has spoken with them and encouraged them, and sometimes helped them to look back on their past earthly lives and see that what matters most on earth is loving and learning, tasks to which they may have to return in a few moments as measured by earthly time.

When the Gospels reach the Resurrection, towards which all they say has been directed, they describe mainly the impact of the event upon human souls, rather than the mysterious process by which the new immortal body beheld by the disciples had been built up. About the process of resurrection in detail we shall need to learn through many centuries. But the Gospels give careful attention, each in its own way to the circumstances and people concerned with the first encounters with the Risen Christ. They are agreed that it was women who saw him first. It was they, with their bodies akin to the more mobile elements, who were sensitive enough to receive such entirely new, unforeseen impressions. And it is the encounter of one very individual woman which is described in the greatest detail.

There is a version of the last chapter of the Gospel of Mark which says of Mary Magdalene that from her Christ had cast out seven demons. Numbers in the New Testament are never accidental. Mary Magdalene has suffered a sevenfold assault through her body upon her soul. Seven is usually a number attributed to good and great heavenly gifts to the earthly world; Genesis begins with the seven days of creation and the whole Revelation to John is built upon the sequence of seven churches, seven seals, seven trumpets and seven vials of wrath. But evils reflect in a distorted form the heavenly order. (Dorothy Sayers invented the consciously awful word 'Lowerarchies'.) The planets have left their imprint in the life processes and organs of the human body, and each of these can be disturbed in ways that trouble the human soul.

These disturbances open the door for dark powers to take possession, dividing the human soul within itself. Many people of the present day experience to some extent such divisions in their personalities; in themselves they are then several, but among other people they are lonely — for no-one knows how to deal with them. Christ has healed Mary Magdalene of this condition, both strengthening her individuality and leading her into the small community of women who lately accompany his journeys, and are near to the Cross. On Easter morning she stays alone near the sepulchre, from which the other women have departed, looking into the darkness, and weeping. She sees two angels in white, 'sitting where the body of Jesus had lain, one at the head and one at the feet'. They ask her why she is weeping, and she speaks of an un-named 'they' who have taken away her Lord. Then she turns away from them and from the darkness of the sepulchre. Now she is looking into the garden at the flowers and shrubs and trees in their spring colours, for it is April. Among them she sees a human being standing, whom she does not recognize. Several times this happens in the resurrection narratives; the form of Christ is not just as it had been before the Passion. He has built up a new body, translucent and immensely mobile, the first member of a new creation of the human being — not from the Sixth Day, but from the First. It is not a pointless mistake that Mary Magdalene supposes him to be the gardener; he has come in order to care for all living things as well as for humanity, and to prevent the earth from becoming a desert.

Mary Magdalene promises him with great courage that if he has taken the body of Jesus, and will tell her where he has laid it, she will carry it away. In answer he speaks her name in such a way that she feels her 'I' addressed and known as only Christ Jesus could do.

Every detail in this conversation calls for long and sensitive thought. It is made more difficult for us by our uncertainties about the full implications of some of the words. *Rabboni* is a fuller, more devoted form of *Rabbi*, and seems

73

generally to have been used for God as teacher. *Rabbi* is sometimes used in St John's Gospel in a somewhat ironic way, with the implication that the speaker does not know that the Christ is much more than the teacher. But here, as used by Mary, it is the complete recognition of the teaching, which she has received from him, healing and purifying her soul. The words now spoken by Jesus have generally been translated 'Do not touch me', following the Vulgate. But there is widespread agreement among modern translators and commentators that she *has* clasped his feet, as the women do in Matthew's Gospel (28:9), and that the Greek word implies holding him back from the further journey which he is making. Instead she is given a task. 'Go to my brethren and say to them, I am ascending to my Father and your Father, to my God and your God.' At the last Supper Jesus had said that he did not call the disciples servants, but friends; now he speaks of them as brothers. And as sister, Mary Magdalene is to join them, turning their minds from the immediate past to the future.

They have great difficulty in believing what is said by her and the other women. But they are beginning to find each other again out of the bitter separateness which they have suffered since the arrest of Jesus. Two other disciples, one of them named Cleopas, walk together on the afternoon of Easter Sunday to the village of Emmaus, north of Jerusalem. It is a progress that they do talk together though still in deep sadness. And a third traveller draws near to them, and walks and speaks with them. With him they go through the sayings in the Law (the Books of Moses), the Prophets, and the Psalms. A glimmer of light penetrates their mind: had it not been foretold that the messenger of God should suffer at the hands of men? At Emmaus they persuade him to enter the house with them. And when the third, whom they had at first regarded as 'a stranger in Jerusalem', at table takes the bread, blesses, breaks, and hands it to them, they recognize him as the Christ, and he vanishes from their sight.

It is to be observed that these appearances of the resurrected Christ come about when for the experience of the disciples there is a mingling of old and new impressions. The two disciples going towards Emmaus have known the passage from the Law and the Prophets all their lives — but now they hear them in a new voice, as if from a stranger, and after great suffering. Similarly, the eleven disciples in the evening are in a familiar place, the Upper Room where the Last Supper had been held and because of feelings derived from the past had secured the house against intruders. But they have new impressions as well; they had heard what the women said, and from Simon Peter that he too had seen the risen Christ, in a meeting not described by the Evangelists. Now the two who had been to Emmaus are admitted and give their testimony. Mysterious though this all is, they are to some extent prepared when the Christ himself stands among them. They believe that they are beholding him in spirit, but he proves to them that he has a physical body though of a new kind; translucent, and immortal, with 'flesh and bones as you see that I have'.

This is from Luke's narrative; there is what may seem a puzzling contradiction with the account given by John. For John says that on that evening Thomas was not with them; how then were they eleven? Perhaps an answer is to be found if we regard the twelve rather less as a fixed group of people and more as a circle reflecting and representing on earth the great heavenly circle of powers which have in the periphery their image in the zodiac. A twelve can be joined by a thirteenth; places in the circle can be taken by different people at different times. John Lazarus, if as seems possible, he was not the same person as John the son of Zebedee, may have joined the rest of the twelve before the Last Supper. There are some ancient pictures which represent thirteen disciples there. But we need not reach a final conclusion about this.

Thus according to John's account Thomas retains a certain sad isolation throughout the first Easter week, unable to believe what the others say. He is a deep melancholic, as his question at the Last Supper illustrates: 'Lord, we do not know where you are going; how can we know the way?' But on the Sunday after Easter the disciples are again in the same place, and the Christ comes to them. After giving them again his blessing of peace he says to Thomas 'Put your finger here, and see my hands; and put out your hand, and place it in my side; do not be faithless, but believing.' When the senses of sight and touch work together, we have in the physical world the strongest assurance of reality. Thomas answers 'My Lord and my God!'

According to John, a third appearance of the Christ to a group of disciples, this time seven of them, was beside the Sea of Galilee. This is told in the twenty-first chapter, which has a quality different from the rest of the Gospel. It has an imaginative, almost dreamlike mood. Physically, the disciples may have all remained in Jerusalem, as seems to follow from St Luke's account. But once more, new experiences, perhaps in the realm of the soul rather than in the physical world, meet with memories from the past. And once more, the Christ is not recognized at first.

Since his denial of his master, Peter carries with him a special grief. The denial was not so dark a trial as the betrayal of Christ by Judas. Even of Judas we should not think that he is condemned after his suicide to loneliness for ever; his soul will rejoin in time the company of servants of Christ. But Peter, though he has already received so much comfort from the fact of the Resurrection, has not yet put behind him all the circumstances of his denial, and of the fierce self-accusation which followed it. Now he is to be directly reminded of these.

During the cold night hours following the arrest of Jesus, Peter had tried to warm himself at a small fire outside the judgment hall of the Sanhedrin. Now there is a similar small fire burning beside the lake, in the first hour of morning. And after they had eaten bread and fishes as the Five Thousand had done in Galilee, Christ Jesus three times questions Peter, using his own name Simon and referring, it seems, to his father: 'Simon, son of John'. Peter has now to make three affirmations as on the tragic night he had three times denied knowledge of Jesus. These affirmations are very difficult for him to make, partly because it is hard for him to see why he should have to do so; surely there could be no question about his love for Jesus. In the Greek of this passage two different words for 'love' are used; and translators have been divided as to whether this variation is significant or not. In his invaluable pocket lexicon to the Greek New Testament Alexander Souter contrasts three Greek words for 'love' giving indications about their use: *eramai* of passionate love, *phileo* of love in friendship, and *agapao* of reverential love. For loneliness, these three seem to work in very different ways. *Eros*, when he is fully ablaze and fully mutual, seems to take away loneliness altogether. But when he departs he may leave behind a still more acute loneliness than before he came. *Philia*, affectionate friendship, is a great and much-needed comfort in loneliness, and can long endure. But the great transformer of painful loneliness into fertile solitude and deep companionship is *agape*, selfless love. In the first question of Jesus to Peter, the verb *agapao* is used; and Peter humbly replies with *phileo*; has not Jesus indeed called him 'friend'. It is the same with the second question and answer, but with the third question Jesus comes down, as it were, in the scale of love, and uses *phileo*. This

is very hard for Peter to bear; is even this degree of
love in him called in question? Thus the passage can be
rendered:

Jesus said to Simon Peter, 'Simon, son of John,
do you love me more than these do?'
He replied, 'Yes, Lord, you know that you are
dear to me.'
Jesus said to him, 'Feed my little lambs.'
Then he said to him again, the second time,
'Simon, son of John, do you love me?'
He replied, 'Yes, Lord, you know that you are
dear to me.'
Jesus said to him, 'Shepherd my little sheep.'
Then he said to him for the third time, 'Simon,
son of John, am I dear to you?'
Peter was grieved that he said to him the third
time 'Am I dear to you?' and he said to him,
'Lord, you know everything. You are aware that
you are dear to me.'
Jesus said to him, 'Feed my little sheep.'*

Peter's temperament impels him to rush into action, and
also to hold back from it; he will only keep steady through
the trials that are to meet him with the help both of the
great divine love and of deep affection. The congregations
he will be called to serve are pictured first as fishes to be
caught in the unbroken net of divine wisdom and then
as sheep. Sheep and lambs are always used in the New
Testament not in the modern sense of thoughtless
imitators, but of beings capable of self-sacrifice in freedom.
It is a noble community into whose service Peter is to grow,
as fisher and shepherd, for the rest of his life.

---

* John 21:15–17. Kalmia Bittleston's translation (Floris Books 1984). William
Temple in his *Readings in St John's Gospel* gives a translation which makes similar
distinctions.

It is only Luke, in the first chapter of the Acts of the Apostles, who gives a full account of the Ascension. The very idea of the Ascension of Christ is full of puzzles for most present-day people. Looking upwards from the earth are we not gazing only into limitless empty space, through which some relatively tiny physical objects are moving at hardly imaginable speeds? And did not the Christ promise that he would stay on earth with his disciples to the end of the world? What can it mean, that 'a cloud took him out of their sight'? Clouds are studied today simply as interesting physical phenomena or as indications about the weather. We think rarely of how much we owe them — without clouds there would be no life on earth — or of the tremendous wealth of movement going on within them. All four elements play a part in their making: earth in the form of specks of dust, water rising as vapour with the help of warmth, and air that forms and moves them. Water that falls from the clouds as rain or snow is by no means just the same as it was when it rose from the earth. It has been regenerated by the elemental beings and brings blessing.

But the earth is not always capable of receiving this blessing in the right way. Heavy rain may wash away the soil, or sink too deeply into the ground unless there are enough trees. Trees slow down the passage of the water, keeping it back with their roots, which go deeper than those of grass or small plants, and hold and enrich the soil. Civilizations can be rescued by the planting of trees. An outstanding example is the olive-tree. The Greeks cut down too many of the trees which covered the mountains of Attica, probably for firewood, houses, and ship-building. Plato describes in the *Critias* how there had been 'tall cultivated trees in abundance, and the mountains afforded pasture for countless herds,' but after the trees were lost, there was severe erosion 'so that what is now left . . . compared with what existed then is like the bones of a

79

body wasted with disease: the fertile soil has fallen away, leaving only the skeleton of the land.' J. Sholto Douglas and Robert A. de J. Hart, in their vitally important book *Forest Farming*, say, after quoting this passage: 'The Athenians thus, like other nations before and since, were faced with the challenge of an eroded landscape . . . but, unlike other peoples who merely abandoned their ancestral land and moved elsewhere, the Athenians faced boldly up to the challenge and overcame it. They turned away from stock-breeding and grain-growing, the staple pursuits of Greece in that age, and concentrated on the cultivation of the olive and the vine, both of which can grow and even flourish on denuded slopes'.

There were many hills in Judea, terraced for the growing of olives. But the Mount of Olives was not so called without reason. It covers a considerable area, much of it steeply sloping, between Jerusalem and the desert hills to the east. Without its olive terraces, the desert might well have reached to the walls of Jerusalem. Thus it is not just the name of a place, when the Mount of Olives is mentioned in the Gospel. It gave a blessed shelter for great deeds of the Christ. Bethany, where Lazarus was raised from the dead, lies on its eastern slopes not long before the road to Jericho enters the desert. On the western slope of the Mount of Olives looking towards the Temple, Jesus gave his great instruction about the future to some of the disciples, early in Holy Week. But high up on the Mount of Olives, forty days after Easter, many disciples beheld him taken up into the realm of the clouds. The great mediator between heaven and earth enters the realm where the elements meet, to mediate between the powers of the sun and the needs of the earth. The 'heaven' into which Christ goes is not somewhere remote but in the great spiritual weaving which goes on in the whole atmosphere of the earth. He blesses now the life of every land, strengthening and guiding the elemental beings in their work to prevent the earth falling into dust too soon. From the heights he now sends gifts to his disciples, which they can only receive through enduring the sorrow of not seeing him any longer in the way that they had seen him since Easter. And at once they receive comfort about the future. 'While they were gazing into heaven as he went, behold two men stood by them in white robes, and said, "Men of Galilee, why do you stand looking into heaven? This Jesus, who was taken up from you into heaven, will come in the same way as you saw him go into heaven" '.

Between the Ascension and Whitsun wonderful human developments go on. The circle of the disciples is completed again; and the family related by blood draws together with the newly instituted spiritual family, so that the Mother of Jesus can be recognized as mother of both. It had been among her many sufferings that her younger sons opposed Jesus before the time of the Passion. The destiny of the eldest of them, 'James the brother of the Lord', only indicated very briefly in the New Testament, has been reconstructed with the help of early Christian traditions by Emil Bock. Like Peter and Thomas, James too had to pass through a dark valley of loneliness.

It was difficult for James to understand Jesus. James was a profoundly religious man, but he developed and retained through life a specially strong attachment to the ancient teachings and practices of the Jews. He could not help regarding the actions of Jesus as expressing a certain disregard for the Law, as did the scribes and Pharisees. Nevertheless it was a great pain for him not to be in accord with Jesus — and this pain increased as the tension mounted in Jerusalem. At the time of the Passion, according to the account of his life given by St Jerome, James resolved to fast in solitude until he was granted light on what had happened. At the end of this time, the risen Christ appeared to him and taught him; and he received the great privilege of celebrating the sacrament of the Eucharist in accordance with Christ's instructions. So the disciples could receive James as they later received Paul, as one they had looked at as remote, who was now their brother. The sacrament of bread and wine could from the time of the Ascension onwards be celebrated anywhere on earth; for the Christ was there already, willing to indwell the pure gifts of earth. The transubstantiated bread and wine could be given to each member of the congregation, as seed in him of the immortal body which is the work of Christ.

A further gift which the disciples could receive after the Ascension, because the visible form of their Lord had gone beyond the limits of their sight, came with the outpouring of the Holy Spirit at Whitsun. Now they became both fully individualities and fully a community, awakening out of the special consciousness which had held them since the night before Good Friday. They could face the world with the confidence that they could bear witness to the Resurrection and find understanding in open human hearts everywhere.

After Whitsun, the appearance of the risen Christ did not cease completely. Saul was an extremely dogmatic Pharisee, expecting the coming of the Messiah to condemn everyone who had not kept the Mosaic Law in scrupulous detail. But after the stoning of Stephen, Saul carried in him a divided soul. Stephen's countenance had shone like that of an angel, he had forgiven his enemies and had seen the Christ in the heights beside the Father. It was not easy to think of him just as a blasphemer. Saul, on his way to Damascus to arrest any Christians he could find there had to leave an infertile region and enter the abundant fertility which surrounded Damascus itself. At noon, when human beings and animals most need the shelter of the trees, Saul had his vision of the Christ, unmistakably the Messiah, but a Messiah who suffers death and does not condemn.

When Paul left Damascus he sought for a time solitude in Arabia, coming back to Jerusalem and meeting the Christians there only after three years. But he did not linger there. His realm was the whole coast of the Mediterranean, the realm, as Rudolf Steiner points out, of the olive tree; and his congregations were found mainly among the Gentiles. When later on tension sprang up about the Mosaic Law between the Gentile Christians and the congregation at Jerusalem, who still kept the Law in its entirety, it was James who was the gentle mediator who spoke the decisive words liberating the Gentile Christians.

6. The presence of Christ today

For nearly two thousand years visions of the risen Christ were rare. But Rudolf Steiner foretold that from about 1933 onwards Paul's vision at Damascus would begin to be renewed for many, increasingly as time went on. By now this promise has been fulfilled, though the examples that have come to be known are comparatively few. Many people have kept silent over years about their experience, or have told it only to people very near them. Accounts written by two remarkable women became widely known. Julia de Beausobre's husband, though of aristocratic descent, had been working as a civil servant when in one of Stalin's purges he was arrested and imprisoned. She too was imprisoned and left in ignorance of her husband's fate. She suffered greatly but forgave her tormentors, and was comforted by the presence of Christ. Her subsequent life bore witness to the genuineness of her experience. The young French writer, Simone Weil, endured great hardship after France was defeated in the Second World War; she too was given a vision of the Christ. More recently a collection of accounts by many people, most of them anonymous, was published in Sweden, edited with great sensitivity by two Swedish theologians, Gunnar Hillerdal and Berndt Gustafsson. Later their book was published in German with an Introduction by Dr Boris Tullander, who refers to what Rudolf Steiner had said. These accounts help us very much to understand what the 'Coming in the clouds' means.

6. THE PRESENCE OF CHRIST TODAY

We have seen that the elemental beings are particularly at home at the borders of things — for instance between earth and water or between water and air, and so on. There are many other bordering spaces, as it were, both in nature and in human life. Not only the elementals are concerned with them; Christ is at work in these frontiers, leaving what is on each side of him free. It is particularly when those who are lonely and distressed come to such frontiers, caring deeply about another person or people or maybe the whole world, that Christ gives the vision of his presence. A chapter of the Swedish collection describes artists, who often stand deeply concerned at the border between the world they perceive and their work. One of them describes Christ's voice in its profound inwardness and goes on to say:

He does not give me fine-sounding explanations
about the world, but he teaches me to understand
the four elements. He explains to me the being of
water, fire, air and earth. He has illumined me
with the light which shines inwardly so that I
cannot forget it . . . He teaches me to understand
the colours and to read in the world of the senses
the language of light. Patiently and tirelessly he
explains it all to me.

Another painter describes an experience of a complex kind. It should perhaps be remembered that what comes to human beings from the realm of spiritual reality can reach them only in ways that are subject to their own condition and their own previous experience; although there is always something fresh and astonishing as well. This painter had worked on a picture containing a few flowers and a fig tree. Then he put away the unfinished picture in a cellar, where it remained for about twenty years. Then he took it out again and began to work further on it, becoming very interested. When it was finished he put it in front of the door of his balcony, and sat down upon the sofa beside the opposite wall.

Then it appeared to me as if Christ's eyes, and his hands too, were moving. The flowers in the garden came to life. They had become human beings who surrounded Christ. Then I saw Christ going with a wavering movement from one side of the picture to the other. Oh, how he spoke! but I took in only one word: 'Gethsemane'. There was a flash of lightning, and Christ disappeared in a light blue mantle. In his place Mary was sitting, clothed in a red mantle, holding a small child in her arms. She and the child moved. A voice said: 'Christ is born again.' Then I saw a flash of lightning, and Christ stood there again. He was speaking constantly, I saw the movement of his lips, but now I was unable to take in any word. All this was repeated several times. First the Christ, and then again Mary with the child.

Many things are remarkable in this account. It has in common with a number of other accounts, that a garden is concerned. It is with a background of trees and moving flowers that Christ appears. Sometimes he is seen with his countenance appearing from a bunch of flowers not rooted in the garden. The artist here *sees* vividly, but grasps only one word. The garden of Gethsemane is at the foot of the Mount of Olives towards Jerusalem, close to the Kidron, a small intermittent stream. The flashes of lightning recall Christ's own words that at his Second Coming he would shine out like lightning from the east to the west. Finally, it seems that some human beings in our century will have as first fruits of reawakening spiritual perception a vision of the Mother. The artist had a subsequent vision in which a child was also concerned. This experience lived on in him strongly through the years.

Often the experience is very much simpler. Sometimes it is only one of seeing, sometimes only of hearing, often of both. A retired man wrote to the Swedish editors of what he had seen as a young man of twenty-two, in about 1923. He had just taken his final school-leaving examination. He fell ill, and his condition threatened his plans for the future. He was depressed and uncertain.

> One night I saw the Christ coming out of the
> darkness. He was striking, but gently shining. He
> bent over me and my bed. He did not resemble any
> of the traditional Christ-pictures. What struck me
> most was the power of his eyes, power and
> gentleness together. Then the picture withdrew
> quietly into the darkness of the wall side and
> disappeared. But in his movement as he withdrew
> there was a strong warning, which I interpreted as:
> 'Seek me.'

Hardly any of the writers of these accounts knew each other or had seen what the others had written. But there is a very strong agreement among them about the quality of the Christ's eyes. They are filled with an inexpressible love. And here we can look back to a great moment in the history of Christianity, when the beloved disciple John was imprisoned on the island of Patmos and probably forced to work in the quarries there. He was separated from the congregation for which he devotedly cared and in all probability from the Mother of Jesus, with whom he lived at Ephesus. He was 'in the Spirit' on a Sunday, when he heard behind him a loud voice like a trumpet. When he turned to see the voice that was speaking to him he saw:

> . . . seven golden lampstands, and in the midst of
> the lampstands one like a son of man, clothed with
> a long robe and with a golden girdle round his
> breast; his head and his hair were white as white
> wool, white as snow; his eyes were like a flame of

fire, his feet were like burnished bronze, refined
as in a furnace, and his voice was like the sound of
many waters; in his right hand he held seven stars,
from his mouth issued a sharp two-edged sword,
and his face was like the sun shining in full
strength.
    When I saw him, I fell at his feet as though
dead. But he laid his right hand upon me, saying,
'Fear not, I am the first and the last, and the living
one; I died, and behold I am alive for evermore,
and I have the keys of Death and Hades . . .'
(Rev. 1:12-18).

The Son of Man has nine attributes, and in every detail
deep meaning is to be found. The fourth is 'his eyes were
like a flame of fire'. Human eyes are wonderfully built 'by
the light, for the light,' but in a way that is hard to grasp
intellectually the eyes may express warmth. Sometimes
human eyes seem coldly objective; sometimes they are both
clear-seeing and warm. The eyes of Christ Jesus as he
approached the tomb of John Lazarus had wept; now they
glow like a flame, seeing. A very lonely person may almost
lose the ability to meet the eyes of another human being;
but the writers of these accounts do not seem to have found
it difficult to meet Christ's eyes, though the light around
him is sometimes described as dazzling. They are willing
that their weaknesses be seen, and know that in this seeing
there is no contempt. Rudolf Steiner said he could give to
a seeking human being nothing more profound than the
words: 'Christ sees us.'

Another account is given by a woman who had experienced a great grief, which filled her mind. She is a devout
traditional Christian, accustomed to pray every morning:
'I thank thee, God, that thou hast kept and protected me
through this night.' But during this difficult time she had
found herself unable to pray, because of all the sadness

occupying her. One morning as she awakened she heard the words: 'Why do you not pray?' She felt these words like a flash of lightning across space. She answered: 'No, I cannot pray now when my mind is full of all this misery.' Then she clearly heard the words: 'Am I unable to go through this, I who am risen from the dead? Every time when light breaks through darkness I rise again, the resurrection happens anew.'

How can a human being face the lightning flash of being completely known? The solitary soul can build a wall around itself, formed out of the sense of guilt. The consciousness of small or great failures becomes a prison. They do not wish to be seen, and the soul behind them hides. This can happen quite seriously as early as adolescence, and even earlier. *Philia* and *agape* can both make their contribution to breaking through this wall.

A very lonely soul may nevertheless have a good friend. But friendships have their vicissitudes. A serious difficulty can arise when the friend asks a question which the lonely one finds it impossible to answer. It is difficult for us to believe that Christ is concerned with our friendships; but he is. This is one of the characteristic moments of distress at a frontier at which his presence may be felt.

In one of the accounts, a hospital nurse describes how on a winter evening in 1940 or 1941 she had revisited her home town and met there an old school friend. One evening they are sitting by the stove, speaking about God. Her friend presses her to tell her something which would strengthen her faith.

> I struggled for words, leant back in my chair, and felt very tired. My tongue could not shape any words. From the dark dining-room behind me something came. I felt as if fire were passing through me. I could not turn my head. I looked straight in front of me, beside the table. Someone

stood for a moment beside me. I saw, although my gaze was fixed rigidly forwards, a form with a robe with many folds. His eyes! They were filled with streaming love. His gaze was strong, firm, and penetrating. Someone remained for a moment in front of me to the side, between my friend and me. My eyes filled with tears and I sat as if seemingly dead. But within me warm life stirred.

Her friend is horrified, calls out her name and begs her to put on the light. She remains very disturbed by what has happened, and feels that neither of them should speak about it to anyone. But the nurse will treasure what has happened all her life. Complete communication about it does not seem to have been achieved between them.

Every encounter with other human beings, even disagreeable ones, is to be taken very seriously, and remembered as clearly as we can. It is a great step towards spiritual awakening when we realize that all these encounters, and what is made of them subsequently, are the concern of the living, present Christ. At the time of the Sermon on the Mount he taught his disciples, 'Love your enemies, do good to those who hate you.' This did not mean a thin, generalized love but something warm, definite, and individual, which includes a willingness to understand how the 'enemy' has become as he is, and of faith in his future. Much in us struggles against this. There is a perceptive English expression 'nursing one's grievances'. We take these prickly creatures into our arms and foster their development. We hinder the approach of other people who may wish to be friendly by describing the behaviour of the 'enemy' in the minutest detail. It is sometimes worth considering how the person, who has seemed so utterly unaccceptable in his behaviour to us, is regarded by other people who have to do with him — his wife, his children, his business associates, his dog . . .

It is the will of the Christ that we should see, and in a sense accept, the thoughts and opinions of others. Every opinion has a certain validity, though it may be extremely difficult to see. Above all, we should not reject opinions because they run counter to the ideas and practices generally accepted in our environment.

The Christ is the great mediator. And he mediates not only between people, but also between different elements in our own being. We are not only what earthly factors, our heredity and our environment, have made of us, but also the unique spiritual individuality which has come from other worlds and other lives, as we have tried to see. Particularly around the age of twenty there can be terrible tensions between the eternal and the everyday elements in us, sometimes leading to dangerous depressions. And in a quite special way Christ seeks to reconcile these elements in our being, so that both learn to accept the other. We have to accept, for example, that we are both town-bred business people belonging to a specific culture *and* creative spirits belonging to the universe.

This work of Christ is not done only for those who acknowledge him or are granted the sight of his presence. Throughout all being he works at frontiers, and within us he works at the frontier between the conscious and the unconscious. None of the kinds of love is wholly either conscious or unconscious; and all of them, including *eros*, are very much Christ's concern. During the day we try to be conscious, helped by the life of the senses; in sleep, though we are largely unconscious, very active impulses are pushing their way upwards, so that we often feel very differently next morning from the day before. Thus it is particularly good to see that the four bridges described earlier are in good repair before we sleep and after waking.

It is at these times, and above all in the early morning that we can prepare our souls for our meeting with Christ

in his full reality. We cannot claim this, but it will come
to us, at some stage of our long journey and we prepare
for it specially by attending to the frontiers of many kinds
which have to be crossed, the gaps in time and space which
have somehow to be filled. Loneliness is the cry coming
from the emptiness of such a gap. We know, and we are
quite right, that we need other human beings spiritually
akin to us. But loneliness can also be an opportunity to
admit our need for other kinds of companionship too: with
animals and plants, with the elemental beings, with those
who have died, with the angels and with the divine Trinity.
The Father works in our depths, the Holy Spirit in our full
consciousness, the Son moves and mediates gently between
all the realms of our being. As we feel that we are called
to all these kinds of companionship, loneliness begins to be
transformed into a deepening of our power to love and an
intensification of our power to learn.

References

Bock, Emil, *Cäsaren und Apostel*, Stuttgart 1978 (5th edn) (English edition in preparation, Floris Books).

Burkhard, Ursula, *Karlik*, Weissenseifen, 1986.

Douglas, J. Sholto, and Robert A. de J. Hart, *Forest Farming*, London 1984.

Hillerdal, Gunnar and Berndt Gustafsson, *Sie erlebten Christus*, Basel 1979.

Julius F. H., 'Nature-Spirits', *Golden Blade 1971*, London 1970.

Lusseyran, Jacques, *And there was Light*, Boston 1963. Reprinted Edinburgh 1985.

Mayer, Johannes, and Peter Tradowsky, *Kaspar Hauser, das Kind von Europa*, Stuttgart 1984.

Ohnuma, Tadahiro, 'Kotodama: The Speech Formation of Japan', *Golden Blade 1984*, London 1983.

Steiner, Rudolf, *The Gospel of St Luke*, London, 1964.

——*Man as Symphony of the Creative Word*, London, 1970.

——*The Spiritual Guidance of Man and Humanity*, New York 1970.

Waterman, Charles (Charles Davy), 'Beethoven's Two Worlds', *Golden Blade 1970*, London 1969.